SO WHAT NOW WHAT

DESIGNING THE NEXT CHAPTER OF YOUR LIFE

BARBARA FAGAN

FOREWORD BY ANNE BRUCE

Niche Pressworks
Indianapolis, IN

SO WHAT, NOW WHAT

Copyright © 2024 by BARBARA FAGAN

All rights reserved. No part of this book may be used or reproduced, distributed, or transmitted in any form or by any means, including photocopying or other electronic methods whatsoever, without prior written consent of the author, except as provided by the United States of America copyright law.

Neither the publisher nor the author is engaged in rendering legal services through this book and shall have neither liability nor responsibility to any persons or entity with respect to any loss or damage caused directly or indirectly by the information in this publication.
For permission to reprint portions of this content or bulk purchases, contact barbarafagan@sourcepointtraining.com

Author Photograph by: Cynthia Glassell

Published by Niche Pressworks; NichePressworks.com
Indianapolis, IN

ISBN
Hardcover: 978-1-962956-06-2
Paperback: 978-1-962956-07-9
eBook: 978-1-962956-08-6

The views expressed herein are solely those of the author and do not necessarily reflect the views of the publisher.

IN LOVING MEMORY

This book is dedicated to the memory of Jim Fagan, my beloved husband of forty-one years. Jim provided me with unfailing love and support to be confident in who I am, to give all of who I am, and to create positive change in the world.

TABLE OF CONTENTS

Foreword	Zaps of Truth	ix
Introduction	I Just Can't Do This...	1

PART 1	**DISCOVERY**	**7**
CHAPTER 1	It's Okay to Be Different	11
CHAPTER 2	Challenging Our World View	25
CHAPTER 3	Letting Go of the Past	41

PART 2	**COMMIT TO TAKING ACTION**	**63**
CHAPTER 4	No Back Doors	67
CHAPTER 5	Clarity of Purpose	85
CHAPTER 6	Accountability — Owning Your Results	105

PART 3	**PUTTING IT ALL TOGETHER**	**117**
CHAPTER 7	Clear Vision and Commitment	121
CHAPTER 8	Communicate to Win	141
CHAPTER 9	Breakdown to Breakthrough	159
CHAPTER 10	Principles of Accomplishment	173
CHAPTER 11	Self-Care During Change	193
CHAPTER 12	The Seasons of Change	209

Endnotes	217
Thank You	219
Meet Barbara Fagan	221
Paying it Forward	223

FOREWORD

ZAPS OF TRUTH

In this book, Barbara Fagan inspires and shares her "zaps of truth" to encourage each person to face change and recognize their resilience and capacity to evolve.

I have known and worked with Barbara for more than a decade. As supporters of each other's work, we have laughed together and cried together. Barbara stands for principles that guide people to take the lead.

Her book is full of practical tools that will empower you to create the next chapter in your life. Barbara writes with a sense of urgency yet patience and commits to sharing the process. All of the building blocks in this book come together to help you create your best self and contribute to the world.

Barbara candidly shares her personal journey of change and many of the client stories that have made her a master coach. She never lets us lose hope and reminds us that we are in control of living, creating, and experiencing the life of our dreams.

I believe you will be inspired to use this book as a field guide and navigational tool through the ups and downs of what life hands you. How you deal with the changes in your life is what matters most. Barbara shows you the pillars of purpose, vision, and core values. She amazingly takes you through the process of change so that you can experience confidence in creating the life you want

—Anne Bruce

ANNE BRUCE

Bestselling author of *Discover True North: A 4-Week Approach to Ignite Your Passion and Activate Your Potential.*

Anne has authored more than 27 books that have helped to guide and inspire the leaders of Fortune 100 and 500 companies worldwide. She is a popular speaker, author, and coach who continues to write bestselling books from her home at the beach in Southern California.

INTRODUCTION

I JUST CAN'T DO THIS...

As the fall of 2019 approached, I knew that it was time to make a change. My husband Jim's health had declined, and he had been diagnosed with dementia and late-onset Alzheimer's. I had a full-time coaching career and a large property to maintain, and I was now also scheduling Jim's more frequent doctor appointments.

I knew it was time to sell our property and find something else for us that required less maintenance. In January 2020, I traveled to Hong Kong, where my coaching team let me know of the great virus in Wuhan, and I quickly made my way homeward. A couple of months later, in the spring of 2020, all of us faced the first realization that this was a global pandemic, and we had no idea how to navigate it.

I continued to prepare the property, taking inventory of what we had and what we would need to begin clearing out.

I called our close friend Ken, who was a broker. I asked him to help me, and we began the appraisal process.

Then, on one clear, sunny, unremarkable day, a large one-hundred-plus-year-old oak tree gave way and suddenly fell, landing on the side of our house and creating a great deal of damage. It was that night, at 1:00 a.m., when I could not sleep, that I called my close friend Dana, crying, "I just can't do this anymore."

To say that I was overwhelmed is an understatement. The accident, coupled with no longer having a spouse who could help solve problems, left me feeling very vulnerable and alone. As a professional coach and friend, I have always been known as strong, grounded, confident, and capable of dealing with every situation. I've helped clients through some very challenging times in their lives, but this was like being hit by a brick.

Dana immediately flew out from the Midwest and stayed with me for two weeks. We created a checklist and began to sort things out — filing an insurance claim, handling bids for the repairs, meeting with Ken to list the property, and a myriad of other things that I had not managed to address.

Together, we began to look at places to move in our area. Jim and I had lived in Healdsburg for almost thirty years, so I wanted to be able to stay in our community of friends, and because of Jim's condition, I wanted to maintain as much familiarity as possible.

Within weeks, we had an offer on our house. I soon found us another home to buy, and I began to plan the move. Two weeks before we moved into our downsized property, excited to have a simpler life, Jim was diagnosed with lung cancer. I was devastated. I felt an urgency to move and get settled in, knowing that our hospital and doctor visits would be taking even more of our time. Most importantly, I wanted Jim to feel the comfort of home and familiar surroundings in the months he had left.

Once in our new home, I prayed that we would have at least one year together to create memories that would last me for the rest of my life. One blessing was that, because of COVID, I was able to stay home and no longer had to travel to Asia to work with clients. Instead, everything was online and done remotely.

As each month passed, Jim experienced comfort and joy, watching the golfers from the deck or sitting quietly with me in the sun surrounded by nature. With each new change in his diagnosis, I challenged myself to adapt, always focused on creating the best quality of life for him.

Two years to the day of our move, Jim passed away peacefully at sunset with me by his side.

What I share with you in this book is borne out of my recent life experiences. You may not have lost a spouse, but part of being human is about facing change, which means we may suddenly become members of a "club" we never wanted to be a part of. As I confronted my husband's passing, I didn't know what I would do when he was gone, and then I asked myself the two questions I've often asked clients in difficult situations — So what? Now what?

At some point, all of us will face a difficult decision or unexpected change. Think of just the past few years. We have all experienced some sort of loss — a loss of work, business, relationships, or connections with others. We've also all explored new possibilities in our lives that required us to be open to change.

Think of this book as a resource to help you navigate life when things aren't quite right — when something is occurring in your life that makes you feel out of alignment. Perhaps it's a time when you experience an event that causes you to shift gears. During these moments, it is time to ask questions: So what is happening? How does my life or career need to change? How do I want my life or career to be?

Now what is possible? What change do you want to make now? What can you do? What possibilities are there for you? What will you create that will make a difference and move you forward? What action will you take in the next week, month, or year ahead?

Being open and forward-looking toward your future and what your next chapter might look like requires courage and commitment. The work I have done in over thirty years of coaching has focused on partnering with clients to help them create the change they want in their lives. Too often, people recognize their "So what?" but don't ask the question, "Now what?" Instead, they look away and give up on creating a beautiful future full of friends and a myriad of possibilities.

While some people have done this as a result of COVID, others have used unexpected changes to re-evaluate their lives and decide what is really important to them. They made decisions that supported their family and their values, perhaps moving or changing jobs and spending more time with their family.

My purpose for writing this book is to help you manage through whatever change you may be facing in your life. I am sharing with you the same tools I'm using to design my own "now what?"

The first step in this process involves self-discovery. It helps you identify how you got to where you are and challenges some of your old beliefs about what is possible for you and your life.

The second step looks to your future. You decide what it is you are committed to causing and creating in your life and begin to identify the actions needed to get there.

The last and perhaps most important step requires you to stay committed to your vision by using all the resources around you, communicating with and enrolling others to support you, and using key principles of accomplishment.

I believe life is not over until it is over. When we reach a time or season in our lives and realize a change is needed, then we need to embrace the change and realize that each of us has the capacity to create a new day with new possibilities. This can be a time of renewal, new friends, new adventures, and new learning on how to face our future.

So what change do you want? Now what is possible for your future?

Let's do this together!

PART 1

DISCOVERY

OWNING YOUR STORY IS THE BRAVEST THING YOU WILL EVER DO.

—BRENE BROWN

CHAPTER 1

IT'S OKAY TO BE DIFFERENT

Based on our early childhood experiences and what we are told, we formulate beliefs about ourselves at a young age. We begin to behave in ways that hide our shame or lack of confidence. We establish behaviors that either reinforce what we've been told or hide our fears of being seen in a way that doesn't serve us.

I can still remember my own feelings from this time. Even though I was only six years old, I vividly recall sitting in the first-grade reading circle at the front of the room with other students in my class, waiting for my turn to read a page. As the child next to me read their page with perfection, my face began to get red, knowing that I would be next and not knowing if the word I was looking at was "it" or "at." I felt this confusion and panic every time we had reading circle.

Looking at the words on the page, I knew I had a fifty-fifty chance of getting it wrong and hearing the other children giggle at my mistake. This was the first time I felt like I was different. None of the other students seemed to struggle like me. My parents tried to help by starting a search to find out what was wrong with me, which led to a series of appointments with doctors to check my eyesight, hearing, and basically, my level of cognition.

Up until this time, I had been a happy, playful little girl, but the realization that I was different (in my mind, stupid) set in very hard. I started to keep to myself and can still remember lonely recess times. My shame about not being able to read well had me standing alone on the playground. There was a red brick wall that the sun would hit each morning. This was my wall. I stood there watching the other kids play, and no one invited me to join in. Of course not — because I was stupid.

This went on, and we didn't get any good answers until fourth grade. My teacher, Mrs. Hirsh, told my mother that she had been observing me in class and felt I had indications of dyslexia. She explained to my mother that it had to do with how my brain processed information. At that time, very few people understood what it meant to have dyslexia.

Later that night, my mother told me that Mrs. Hirsh wanted to work with me after school to help me read and understand my assignments better. At first, I felt nervous about having more attention paid to my learning challenges.

However, during my first after-school session with Mrs. Hirsh, she didn't talk to me about my grades or my challenges with homework. Instead, she said that she noticed how hard I was working on my assignments.

She explained that people learn in many different ways. She said, "Barbara, I notice you enjoy art and are quite good at drawing pictures." She shared that some people can see pictures in their minds quite clearly, and other people remember words more easily. She explained that people's brains work differently and take in information differently.

As we worked together each day, I can remember her quiet voice talking softly to me, and I remember how patient she was with me as I read my assignments. I began to see words as pictures in order to remember them and became more confident. I remembered words more easily and was starting to figure out how they were related to one another. I felt the excitement of being able to put words together. From that time on, I began to enjoy reading more. I would sit in my closet, reading books with my flashlight, when I should have been in bed. I read everything I could, from Nancy Drew to Swiss Family Robinson.

While my new reading skills helped me catch on faster in class, I still struggled with learning. My older sister got As and Bs, and I struggled to get Cs. I constantly heard my parents say, "You just need to apply yourself," "You can't be lazy," or "You need to study more." But no matter how hard I tried, didactic learning never came easy to me.

From these early experiences, I began to have certain limiting beliefs about myself. They'd show up at times when I was in situations with others whom I perceived to be more knowledgeable than I was. I had decided I was not smart, and that belief has stuck with me all these years.

As recently as the last six months, this limiting belief has still come up. As I struggled to put our affairs in order after Jim's death, I felt frustrated with myself when talking to my financial planner about how our assets needed to change, when figuring out how to have continued income and security, and when dealing with our attorney about our living trust. My self-doubt and lack of confidence still show up, along with that voice in my head, asking, "What's wrong with me?" or saying, "I'm not smart enough to figure all this out."

We all want to be seen as capable and having value, and we want to be recognized for our contributions. It brings us a sense of self-confidence and fulfillment. Yet often, those early experiences and the emotions of shame (or feelings of embarrassment that accompany them) can stay with us our entire lives. When not recognized or addressed, limiting beliefs can hinder our sense of accomplishment and sense of self.

SELF-LIMITING BELIEFS

What are some of your early childhood experiences? Can you remember times when you felt different or inadequate? We all have these moments buried in our unconscious mind. However, while we may not remember specifics, we remember the emotions associated with those events.

Because of these early experiences, we begin to have beliefs about ourselves and how we should be. After thirty-plus years of coaching people, I have heard them all. People were told:

- Don't be so loud.
- Don't be so quiet.
- Don't be selfish.
- Don't be weak.
- Don't be lazy.
- Don't be a coward.
- Don't be so controlling.

As we get older, we take these early childhood experiences and turn them into the negative self-talk that we hear when we are in a new experience, under stress, or feeling tested by others:

- I'm not smart enough.
- I'm not strong enough.
- I'm not loving enough.
- I'm not pretty enough.
- I'm not brave enough.
- I'm not ... you name it.

These self-limiting beliefs show up at times when we are under stress or are feeling inadequate. The warning signs are always there. You are feeling doubtful and don't trust yourself. You may be feeling threatened by others. You may feel hopeless or lack self-confidence. Even though we would do almost anything to stop these beliefs and the nagging voice that tells us we are different or not enough, it seems as if we are powerless to quiet them.

Limiting self-talk affects our identity. Even when we are successful in business and in relationships, this type of self-talk can sabotage our sense of accomplishment and fulfillment. Clare Josa, researcher and author of *Ditching Imposter Syndrome*, says men with imposter syndrome are more likely to push through it. Women, on the other hand, are more likely to let imposter syndrome stop them from taking opportunities to shine or going for promotions.[1]

How we **see** ourselves is not who we **are**. We all feel like imposters at times. This comes from growing up being told things like study hard, please people, be nice, work hard, be successful, get good grades, be the best, etc. When we actually achieve success, many of us still feel like we are not good enough or that there is more we should be doing.

Growing up, my youngest sister, Debbie, and I were best friends. We would often talk about our early childhood memories, especially as they pertained to our parents. Families tell their stories, and very often, siblings from the same family tell very different stories. Debbie would recall an event in an entirely different way than I would remember it. I believe our different perspectives had a lot to do with our place in the family — our birth order. As the middle child, I was usually seen as the rebel, always testing the boundaries. Debbie was the youngest and usually seen as obedient (she learned by watching her older siblings what worked and what didn't work with our parents).

But I think it's about more than birth order. Our memories are also tempered by the roles we assumed — the labels we were assigned, like "rebellious" or "obedient." The messages these send are hard to shake, and we often carry them with us into adulthood, where they can become self-limiting beliefs.

WHO YOU ARE IS WHERE YOU WERE

Years ago, I attended a lecture where the speaker talked about "who you are" being connected to "where you were when." That statement made an impression on me, and I reflected on how my life experiences had shaped my beliefs.

One of my early memories was when John F. Kennedy was shot in 1963 and the realization that our President was not safe. When the Kent State riots, protesting the Vietnam War, happened in May 1970, it was a watershed moment. I remember thinking, "What will it take to end this terrible war? So many of my generation are losing their lives — and for what purpose?" In 1972, when the Watergate break-in occurred, I remember thinking, "Can we trust our government?" And then, on the morning of September 11, 2001, I got a call from my son telling me to turn on the TV, and as I watched the Twin Towers in New York City collapse, I thought, for the first time, "We are not safe."

For every generation, events like these shape our beliefs and, subsequently, the way we behave. They change the way we see the world and change many of the choices we make going forward.

When I listen to my clients share their experiences, rather than analyzing what they are sharing with me, I see their story. I hear how these experiences have affected them, and I can feel the burden they carry in trying to measure up to everyone's standards of how they are supposed to be. But remember what we talked about at the beginning of this chapter — it's okay to be different. You don't have to live up to anyone else's expectations.

BEING DIFFERENT – OWNING YOUR AUTHENTICITY

Each of us has unique gifts that come from a combination of our DNA and our life experiences. These formulate who we become. Just as each person has their own unique fingerprint, unlike anyone else's, we each have our own contribution to make by being authentically who we are.

In Anna Quindlen's book *A Short Guide to a Happy Life*, she shares her high school experience of striving to be perfect

JUST AS EACH PERSON HAS THEIR OWN UNIQUE FINGERPRINT, UNLIKE ANYONE ELSE'S, WE EACH HAVE OUR OWN CONTRIBUTION TO MAKE BY BEING AUTHENTICALLY WHO WE ARE.

and how she came to realize when she was at Barnard College that trying to be perfect was like "carrying a backpack filled with bricks." She invites her reader to make choices that reflect "who and what I am."[2]

Discussing his new daytime television show, Anderson Cooper told *The Vancouver Sun*, "In everything I've done, I've always tried to just be authentic and real." And Sarah Ferguson, Duchess of York, shared that "if you fear what people think about you, then you are not being authentic."[3]

At the same time, legions of marketers and social networking coaches are preaching that to succeed online — on Twitter, Facebook, Instagram, Match.com, etc. — we must all "be authentic!" On dating sites like OKCupid, the word pops up with remarkable frequency in people's descriptions; on eHarmony.com, users can browse dating tips, where they are advised that in a healthy relationship, "both individuals feel free to be authentic."

Sarah Ban Breathnach's *Something More: Excavating Your Authentic Self* challenges each of us to be an archaeologist of our own selves by delving into our past and excavating the authentic woman buried inside.[4]

My sister and I became followers of Sarah's philosophy when she wrote her first book, *Simple Abundance: A Daybook of Comfort and Joy*. Her work has inspired hundreds of thousands of women of every age to redesign how they see themselves and the world around them.

Learning to be authentic takes time because we must be willing to look at all parts of ourselves. This usually starts in midlife when we begin to focus on personal growth and self-awareness.

In *The Velveteen Rabbit*, author Margery Williams writes this about authenticity:

> "Real isn't how you are made," said the Skin Horse. "It's a thing that happens to you when a child loves you for a long, long time, not just to play with, but REALLY loves you, then you become Real."
>
> "Does it hurt?" asked the Rabbit. "Sometimes," said the Skin Horse, for he was always truthful. "When you are real, you don't mind being hurt."
>
> "Does it happen all at once, like being wound up," he asked, "or bit by bit?"
>
> "It doesn't happen all at once," said the Skin Horse. "You become. It takes a long time. That's why it doesn't happen often to people who break easily, or have sharp edges, or who have to be carefully kept. Generally, by the time you are real, most of your hair has been loved off, and your eyes drop out and you get loose in the joints and very shabby. But these things don't matter at all, because once you are Real, you can't be ugly, except to people who don't understand."[5]

Discovering your authentic self requires a commitment to developing yourself. Like musicians and athletes, you must devote yourself to a lifetime of realizing your potential.

We spend so much of our time trying to be like everyone else or comparing ourselves to others that we forget to invest time and energy into finding out authentically who we are and what we want. Many times, in midlife or after a significant life-changing event, people begin to ask themselves the question, "Who am I?" and "What is important to me?" These questions lead to the beginning of real-life changes.

When coaching people, I work to help them become aware of and let go of their self-limiting beliefs. This clears the space and makes room where people can begin to create something new. Holding on to old beliefs prevents us from experiencing who we are authentically without judgment. Just because things have been the way they were in the past doesn't mean we can't evolve and grow and discover more of who we can be in the future.

IS IT TIME FOR A NEW CHAPTER?

Knowing when it is time to begin a new chapter in life is a very personal choice. It usually comes at a time when we are feeling unfulfilled or have experienced a loss of some sort — loss of a job, a relationship, finances, our health, etc.

There is a general sense of being unsettled, lacking motivation, or having lost interest in our lives. If you are feeling this way, here are some questions to ask yourself:

- What is missing for me in my life right now?
- What is the mood that I am feeling right now?
- What is incomplete in my life right now?
- What is calling me right now?
- What do I want in my life right now?

By examining these questions, you will begin to see what is needed in order to start making changes in your life. This is perhaps the first step to self-discovery — beginning to evaluate what and where you want to go next. It is a good time to seek counsel or coaching to assist you in designing and navigating this new chapter.

As you begin this process, you will need to examine your beliefs and world view. You'll need to challenge the way you see things and let go of the ways they have always been. A fresh perspective can help you see new possibilities and make shifts in your attitudes and behaviors so you can begin to develop new capabilities.

MAKING CHOICES BASED ON YOUR PAST IS LIKE DRIVING YOUR CAR, ALWAYS LOOKING IN THE REAR-VIEW MIRROR; IT STOPS YOU FROM SEEING WHERE YOU ARE GOING.

CHAPTER 2

CHALLENGING OUR WORLD VIEW

Our world view is like a map. It is based on our beliefs, attitudes, and assumptions, though not necessarily on reality. We make our choices based on our map, which reflects how we view the world and what we think is possible. Learning to shift your world view opens new possibilities.

Kevin Fagan is Jim's youngest brother by ten years. Being the youngest, Kevin was influenced by what his older brothers thought. Just before Kevin was about to graduate from Sacramento State University, Jim took a trip to visit him. Kevin was only twenty years old and a bit socially awkward. Jim wanted to support him as an older brother.

Jim asked, "Hey Kevin, what are your plans after you graduate?"

Kevin thought for a minute and shared, "Well, I guess I am going to be a history teacher, but I don't have a real plan set up yet."

"Is that what you would really like to do?" Jim asked.

Kevin then shared that for the last year, he had been contributing to the college paper by creating some cartoons. "I really have fun with it, sharing cartoons that reflect what college kids are going through. Everyone really seems to like it."

Jim asked, "Who are your favorite cartoonists?"

Kevin thought for a minute and said, "Of course, Charles Shultz, who does *Peanuts*, everyone loves him. And Bil Keane, who writes *Family Circus*, actually comes to the Ivy House in Laguna Beach where Mom works. She has told him that I like to do cartoons, and he told Mom that he would be happy to talk with me about it."

A few weeks after this visit, Kevin got a letter from Jim. Jim told him that he had been thinking a lot about their visit and what Kevin had shared about doing cartoons.

Jim said, "I know Mom and Dad raised us in our faith to always be in service and find ways to contribute to others. There are many teachers and professors, and of course, that is a great way for people to contribute." He then went on to share a scripture that says, "In order to do God's work, we must use the gifts that God has given us." Jim asked, "Don't you think that bringing humor and joy to people are your gifts to contribute to others? Not everyone has this unique talent as a way to contribute."

After Kevin read the letter, he thought about it and decided to take a big risk and send some of his cartoons off to Charles Shultz and Bil Keane. He called Jim a few weeks later and shared, "I heard from Charles Shultz. He looked at my strips, and he said he thinks I have talent."

Within two months, Charles introduced Kevin to the publishers at United Feature Syndicate in New York City, one of the largest cartoon syndication services in the country. Now twenty-one and a college graduate living at home, Kevin flew to New York City to meet with the publishers at United Feature. He was sitting outside their offices waiting to meet with them and thought, "What if I fail at this? The whole world will know it!"

He didn't fail. In fact, within the next few weeks, he was discussing a ten-year contract. It was very exciting, but the realization that he would be required to write a strip every day for the next ten years felt overwhelming. "What if I can't do it?" he thought.

Then he remembered the meeting with Bil Keane that his mom had set up. Bil had said, "You know the really good cartoonists are always there to support new people coming up, and you can count on me for any help you may need." He had heard the same thing from Charles Shultz. Whatever he needed, he just needed to ask for it and have faith and trust that he was doing the right thing.

Two months later, Kevin Fagan signed a contract and launched the strip *Drabble* with United Feature Syndicate. In March 1979, at the age of twenty-two, he was featured in *People* magazine as one of the youngest syndicated cartoonists in the country.

Four years later, his mom, Billie, became ill with breast cancer. Kevin continued to write a strip each day for eight months while supporting her. He took her for medical treatments and visited her in the hospital each day until she died in August 1983. What kept him going was remembering that he had a gift and a responsibility to contribute that gift, even in the face of difficult personal circumstances.

Kevin was willing to challenge his world view, be open to a new possibility, and take "the road less traveled," as Dr. Scott Peck shares in his book of the same name.[6]

Kevin went on to raise three wonderful children and found a way to write his strip each day. Charles Shultz (aka Sparky) was his mentor until the day he died.

Today, Kevin spends time talking to people and sharing his experience, with the hope that he can be a positive influence on others the way his brother and mentors were for him. It is because he trusted himself enough to challenge his world view and the way he thought his life was supposed to look that he has been able to impact the lives of thousands of people each day as they read their *Drabble* comic strip.

Acknowledging Your World View

For over thirty years as a coach, I have worked with clients to help them challenge their world views. In the discovery phase of coaching, I sit with clients to listen and understand their world view — the filters through which they perceive things. I want to know what is truly important to them, what vision they have for themselves, and what new possibilities they want to explore. Are they interested in making a radical change in their life, or do they just want to make adjustments because of certain circumstances?

I recently started working with a middle-aged man who wanted to change his life completely. He said to me, "I want to change everything in my life."

"Everything?" I asked curiously.

"Yes, everything," he replied.

As a coach, I have learned not to ask an open-ended "why?" question when what I really want to know is the underlying reason for this radical change. Instead, I ask if there is a specific event that has led to this conclusion. It could be that they have ended a relationship, lost their job, or had a health scare.

Over the next few months, he began to realize that he had never trusted himself to change his life, and now, in middle age, he feared that he had missed out on many opportunities. He was afraid that if he didn't make a radical change right then, he would go to his grave, regretting all the things he had never done.

As we worked together, he discovered that he really didn't need to make a radical change but, instead, had to give himself permission to be spontaneous, learn new things, and meet new people. From this self-awareness, we began to design a new chapter, where he would explore new possibilities and begin to create a life that brought him more fulfillment and joy.

Most people don't realize that they have a fixed view of the world. By that, I mean that they think the way they think, seldom challenging their assumptions and interpretation of the world. They go through life with a set notion of how they should be and how life should be — go to school, get a job, get married, have children, raise kids, manage bills, contribute to their community, etc., and hope to retire someday and be able to relax and enjoy their families and friends.

The older I get, the more I notice that I take time to read the obituaries. I think about each person as the points of their life are shared with the world after they are gone. For those who are older and have passed, I wonder if they had all that they wanted in life. Did they give all that they wanted in life? What would they have done differently?

I realize that there is no "normal" to life. Each person's life is a journey, and it is shaped by how they see the world. Understanding and acknowledging this world view is the first step toward opening oneself to new possibilities.

Impact of World View

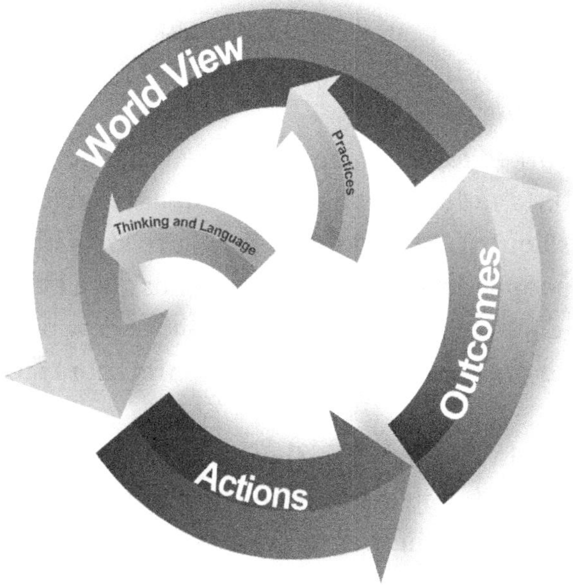
World View
Practices
Thinking and Language
Outcomes
Actions

WORLD VIEW – A MAP OF YOUR REALITY

A world view is like a map of how we interpret and navigate our lives. Our world view is comprised of our many life experiences and perspectives. We begin to shape our beliefs when we are young. The environment in which we are raised teaches us how

A WORLD VIEW IS LIKE A MAP OF HOW WE INTERPRET AND NAVIGATE OUR LIVES.

things are. It may not always be pleasant, but we move forward and learn about life based on our experiences over many years as we grow and learn. I certainly am not a psychologist, but I have learned from years of coaching that people either want to grow up to be just like the family they were raised in or they want their lives to be completely different.

Components of Your World View

The following components of a world view can predict the way you speak, the practices and behaviors you embrace, and ultimately, the choices you make and the results you have.

Your vision and sense of what is possible – How you approach your life and look to your future impacts your world view. Some people avoid looking to the future because their immediate circumstances are so all-consuming that they can't imagine anything beyond their current circumstances. Others see the future through rose-colored glasses and feel that there are abundant possibilities.

Your goals and objectives – Having specific goals and objectives will dictate the way you plan your time and influence your behavior and the actions you take. Some people regularly develop short-term goals, perhaps for the year ahead. Seldom do they create long-term goals, especially in today's world, where there seems to be so much change and ambiguity.

Your immediate circumstances – What seems to be most important at the moment is usually based on your current circumstances, and this dictates your behavior and attitudes.

For example, if you are a new mother, then your time and focus will be spent on your child, developing a new rhythm for your family to adjust to. If you have changed jobs, your time and attention will be focused on getting settled, meeting new people, and learning new systems or processes for work.

Your beliefs and values – You develop your beliefs and values at a young age, largely influenced by immediate family members and events. As you get older, you begin to challenge certain things (hence the teenage years of testing and, sometimes, rebellion). As we begin to create our own identity and how we want to live, we somewhat unconsciously create our own value frame. As a coach, it is important for me to understand and respect my client's values. In fact, the more I can encourage my clients to live aligned with their values, the more at peace they are with themselves and the more effective they are at having others respect their values.

Your frame of mind – What is the mood or attitude you bring to life each day? Are you joyful, scattered, tired, serene, calm, skeptical, or filled with resignation or guilt? Our mood and frame of mind shape our reality and how we respond to the world around us in different situations. I often will say to my clients, "Change your attitude, and your experience of a situation will change as well."

How you make decisions – Some of us are planners, some are not. And some of us are spontaneous, while others find spontaneity difficult or stressful. The way we approach things is based on how we see the world and the way our brains process information. Left-brain thinkers like to have a plan and analyze information to see what is possible. Right-brain thinkers tend to rely on instinct and their gut when deciding to make a change.

Your background and culture – Your personal, social, and cultural experiences in life influence your behaviors and personal practices. This can go as far as predicting your daily routine. For example, daily prayer, morning exercise, timing for meals, family traditions and rituals, etc.

All of the above factors combine and interact to create your world view. They drive the choices you make and the actions you take. Learning to understand your world view is something that most people don't spend enough time developing, so it's not surprising when they are also unaware of other people's world views.

Most of us listen to people through the lens of our own world view without considering the world view of the person with whom we're interacting. This often leads to a right/wrong or good/bad perception based on how we interpret what we hear. But, if we take time to explore our own world view, it can help us better understand another person's perspective. It teaches us to listen deeply so we are able to hear what is really important to them.

What I always remember about Jim's conversation with Kevin is that he asked questions and was able to listen and understand what was important to Kevin. He was able to encourage Kevin to reflect on how he truly felt and think about what would really bring him joy and a sense of contribution. He remained curious and offered suggestions.

Jim just as easily could have urged his brother to stay on a track that was very predictable and secure. However, that would have never allowed Kevin to challenge his beliefs about what he thought he was supposed to do and explore new possibilities. As a result, Kevin was able to realize his gifts were unique and could make a great contribution to people's lives.

In the early days of the pandemic, I heard so many people say, "I will be so glad when this is over and we can get back to normal." Having worked for many years with clients to help them manage change, I had an instinct that after COVID, there would be no "going back to normal." We would all change. Our daily practices would change. Our systems and the way we interacted would change. Some of this change might be for the better, but some of it would not.

In the first six months of COVID, I witnessed many people reacting to the changes based on their world view (aka map). "How can they close the schools? What am I supposed to do with my kids?" or, "How can they close all the businesses? Where will I go to shop?" and even, "I don't know how to cook. Where will we go to eat?" While so many people were trying to maintain a sense of normalcy, it soon became clear that there was no longer any normal.

COVID required all of us to navigate tremendous changes. As we begin to reenter our lives and move forward, we will continue to have our world view maps challenged in new ways.

BELIEFS, ATTITUDES, AND ASSUMPTIONS

Our world view is based on our history and past experiences — not necessarily on what is happening in our life today. When faced with change that we feel we cannot control, we will hold on to anything that gives us a sense of power over our environment. During COVID, many people began to create their own cocoon to try to manage the uncertainty. Home improvement prices skyrocketed, and everything was backlogged. Home garden supplies and plants became the new favorite pastime.

My life has changed, along with the lives of my friends and community. We have all had to create a new map and find new ways to navigate our lives. For many, like myself, there has been a loss of identity. There are still days when I ask myself, "Who am I now?" and I feel the sadness and loss of being alone. Single people were not able to go out and socialize the way they had been accustomed to, often making them feel lonely and isolated. Couples who had wedding plans in progress had to pivot and choose to either forgo the grand celebration with all their loved ones present or delay it until some unknown point in the future. People who worked from home missed the day-to-day interaction with their co-workers and lost a sense of connection. Many workers are still experiencing this today. We all have something in common, though — we didn't see it coming. We all had assumptions about what our life was going to be like in that period, and we were blindsided.

As I have gotten older, I see more of my mother in myself. I catch myself looking at millennials and Gen Z and being critical of what I sometimes perceive as a lack of responsibility. Compared to my generation, it seems they are taking life too easy and not working hard enough or pushing themselves. But when I talk with my grandsons, nieces, and nephew, I realize that they have different world views. They watched their parents take the road of hard work and no play (some were latchkey kids), and now, most of them have decided that this is not the path they want to take. Different generations, different world views — who's to say what is right or wrong?

After asking ourselves, "So what is happening? Now what is possible?" we can begin to create a new version of our lives, one where we understand our world view, embrace our values, and live with a sense of purpose. This takes work, but it is the only thing that will empower us to move forward. Without clarity and a sense of purpose, we can remain stuck and live in the past, holding on to our memories and never being able to see a future. As a committed listener and coach, I work with people to help them realize that they always have the power to move forward and that the only way out of their present circumstances is to work through them.

WHAT SHAPES YOUR WORLD VIEW

- **What is your vision and sense of what's possible for the future?** How are you approaching your life plans? For instance, is it with optimism (the possibilities are endless) or pessimism (life will be more of the same; it is hard)? Find examples of times when you decided to make a change. What were your thoughts and behaviors?
- **What are your goals and objectives?** What plans do you have for your life right now? What about in the next month or the next year?
- **What are your immediate circumstances?** What is occupying your thoughts right now? Where and how are you spending most of your time? What fires are burning?
- **What are your beliefs and values?** What area of your life do you value most? Health? Relationships? Cite examples of how you navigate this area of your life based on your beliefs and values.
- **What is your frame of mind?** What is your current frame of mind? What is influencing this mood? Is it positive or negative?
- **What are the ways you make decisions?** How do you approach choices in your life? Do you tend to be certain or spontaneous? How do you respond to what people think of your decisions?
- **What history and culture frame the way you see your life?** What are some of the practices — social and cultural — that you bring into your daily life?

WE MUST LET GO OF THE LIFE WE PLANNED, SO AS TO ACCEPT THE ONE THAT IS WAITING FOR US.

—JOSEPH CAMPBELL

CHAPTER 3

LETTING GO OF THE PAST

We all like to remember things the way they were. Even if things in the past were not always great, they were at least familiar. But change cannot happen if you hold too tightly to the past. It takes courage to let go, so let's talk about letting go and planning how to move forward.

Oftentimes, we hold on to what we know, convincing ourselves that it isn't that bad. Or we wait for things around us to change so we don't have to change them ourselves. Many of my clients take this approach, saying, "Someday, when I have the money or the time or the kids are older, then I will make the change."

Once we start thinking about change, it's important to frame it correctly. Many of us talk about what we don't want rather than what we do want. I like to help clients identify and get clear about exactly what it is they want. This means working together to identify future possibilities and then creating a plan to move them toward their goal.

In 2017, there was a fire in Sonoma County, where I live, that destroyed over three thousand homes in the course of forty-eight hours. Since then, fires in California have become more frequent. While people are better prepared for emergencies, the fires still have an emotional, financial, and physical impact on those affected.

I remember sitting in a coffee shop days after the 2017 fire and hearing a woman meeting with her insurance agent say, "I wish I had gone to the dry cleaner that day. Then, at least, I would have some clothes to wear now." Hearing her, it really hit home for me how many people's lives had been changed forever.

A year after the fire, I had an opportunity to work with a woman who had lost her home. She was in the middle of rebuilding, dealing with all the logistics and emotional stress of managing the process. Each week, she faced new challenges — missed deadlines by contractors, shortages of building materials, the additional cost for those scarce materials, and needing to find a house to rent and live in for two years while her home was being rebuilt.

She shared with me that she had a great deal of anger and frustration as well as a feeling of powerlessness. I asked her to share with me memories of the house her family had lost. She told me about family holidays they had celebrated when their children were little and dinner parties with friends and neighbors they had hosted through the years.

Weeks later, we began to discuss what she wanted to bring into the new space they were creating. She said, "I want our house to be filled with love and provide joyful experiences for each person who comes to visit." Before the final walls were put into place, she asked all her family and friends to write a blessing for their new home on a card or piece of paper. She and her husband then took these blessings and placed them on the framework of their home before the drywall and plaster were installed. Now, when I enter her house today, I see the beautiful space and feel surrounded by the love and messages contained in the walls. She was able to let go of her anger, frustration, and powerlessness and create a new home full of joy, healing, and memories (both old and new).

Time to Grieve

When we face a change or loss that we cannot control, healing and living exist simultaneously. While we're spending time healing, we're still moving through the immediate needs of the present. This requires that we give ourselves grace. I am not going to tell you how to deal with grief, even though I now have experienced it. That is a different book. However, any type of dramatic change or loss requires time to heal. And that healing process cannot be rushed. The more time you can give it, the more complete your healing will likely be. You must have a sense of resolution and closure in order to move forward.

Think of your life. What changes have occurred over the last few years? How have they impacted your life today? Some big changes that have a big impact include:

- Loss of job
- Loss of business

- Loss of relationship
- Loss of a loved one
- Loss of social community
- Loss of finances
- New relationships
- New job
- New locations to live or work

When encountering changes like these, there are very specific stages people go through. First, depending on the circumstances, it is common to feel either resistance or optimism. If this is a change you are choosing, it is more likely you will feel optimistic in the beginning.

This reminds me of when I changed from a Windows-based computer to an Apple MacBook. While not a huge life change, it illustrates the resistance and optimism that are part of the change process. At first, I was excited. There were so many more things I could do with my MacBook. I also wouldn't need to worry so much about viruses. When my new MacBook finally arrived, I arranged to have all my files moved from the PC to the Mac.

Once everything was in place, I was excited to get started, but that excitement soon faded. "What? Files aren't saved the same way?" I can't tell you how many files I lost in the first week. My optimism about the Mac's amazing benefits soon turned to resistance. I started getting frustrated, realizing that the transition would not be as easy as I thought and would take more time than I thought. Eventually, it worked out, but there were bumps along the way.

This process holds true for change of all types. We need to learn to be open to the change that is occurring. When coaching, I ask clients, "What do you want, and how will you know when you have achieved it?" It's essential to clearly define the type of change you want and what it will look like when you achieve it. Once this is established, it's easier to be open to and accepting of the change process.

CHANGE REQUIRES ACTION

Any type of change is going to require you to take action — action that is consistent with what you say you want. As you take action and begin to see results, you gain more clarity and have the confidence to make decisions about how to move forward.

The empowerment that you start to feel will help you actually achieve the goals you want. This is where coaching can be useful. A coach is a committed partner who will work with you during every step of the change process. Coaches remind you of what you say you want and encourage you to keep moving forward, even when you just don't feel like it.

Stages of Change

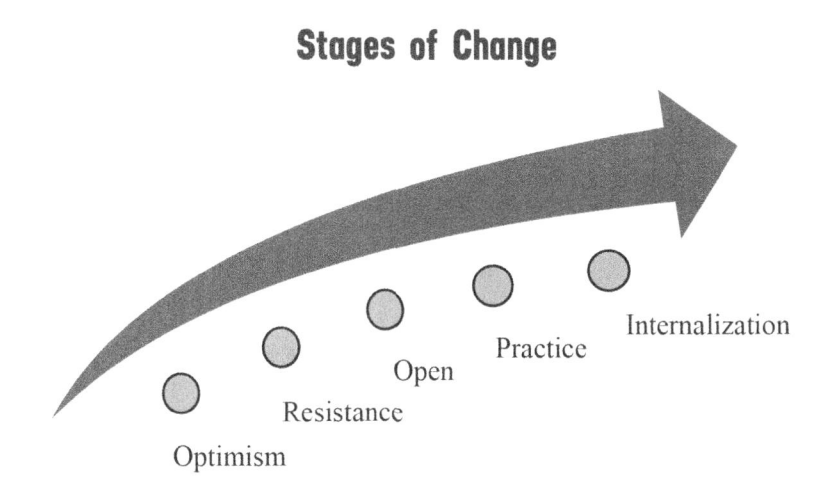

Optimism → Resistance → Open → Practice → Internalization

ANY TYPE OF CHANGE IS GOING TO REQUIRE YOU TO TAKE ACTION

Stages of Change

When a change occurs, there are very specific stages we go through. It helps to understand that at the start, you're likely to feel optimistic, but at some point, you will begin to feel resistant to the change. Which stage you're in (optimistic or resistant) influences your attitude, reactions, and behaviors. Once you move past resistance and commit, you can start creating something new in your life.

By understanding what happens at each stage in the change process, we can develop effective ways to move forward and attain our goals. The five stages of change include:

Stage 1 – Optimism. You are feeling excited about creating something new and are eager to begin facing change and seeing new opportunities. You are not yet aware of the potential barriers to success that you might face.

Stage 2 – Resistance. Even if you are taking on change and seeing the positive benefits for yourself, you will feel resistance at some point — often when you first realize that what you want to create is not going to be easy. This is because making changes in your life requires you to do something differently, learn something new, behave in new ways, and perhaps be in a new environment.

You will be faced with challenges, and when resistance comes up, your commitment will be tested. At this point, you will have to decide whether you are committed to the change. You may decide that you are unwilling to invest the time and energy to practice and learn what is needed in order to create the change you want.

Stage 3 – Openness. Once you have moved past your resistance, you begin to see new possibilities and become open to working through what is needed. In order to realize the benefits of the change you are involved in, you must stay open. Being open keeps you moving forward rather than giving up. To manifest the change you want, you will have to get curious, seek advice or support, and ask questions to understand what is needed to achieve success. You may still feel some resistance at times, but you are beginning to see the benefits and value that lie ahead.

Stage 4 – Practice. It is said that it takes at least twenty-one days to create a new habit that feels like a natural part of your life. As you navigate the process of change, it's important to put consistent practices in place to help change attitudes or behaviors. When you commit to these practices, you'll begin to see signs of the change you want and will be able to envision your desired outcomes. You will gain new capabilities and an increased sense of self-confidence.

Stage 5 – Internalization. With any change, if the attitudes, behaviors, and structures are in place for twenty-one-plus days, then internalization can occur. At this point, you no longer need to stop and think about what you are doing. The behaviors have become second nature. You have the ability to respond automatically and have the capability to generate consistent results in this new chapter of your life.

As we move through these stages of change, we are beginning a new phase of life. This transition puts us in learning mode and can feel overwhelming. Our brains are conditioned to sort information into known and unknown categories. But when we start something new, everything is different, and "we don't know what we don't know." This can be very unsettling.

Part of the transition process may involve finding a new system for organizing information. When I start a new Professional Performance Coach Certification course, I make sure to let students know that they will learn new theories and philosophies. Their brains may not know how to associate and store this information. I encourage them to think of their brain as a large refrigerator with many different compartments where they can store different types of food. If they find that they can't figure out where to store some of the information, I invite them to just let it sit out on the counter, figuratively. Eventually, they will find a place to store it.

GETTING CLEAR ABOUT WHAT YOU WANT

When preparing to move forward in your life, take time to reflect on where you are now and what changes you want to make. Consider the following questions. There are no right answers, and your responses may surprise you.

- In what area of your life would you like to make a change?
- What's possible for you right now?
- What do you want?
- What would having what you want create for you?
- How would you know when you created what you want?
- How would your life change?
- What new skills or capabilities will you need?

- What resources do you have?
- How can you enlist others to support you by asking for what you want — not waiting for it to come to you?
- What would be the first step you could take?

Reflect on your responses to these questions to help focus on what you want now and in the future.

When thinking about making changes in our lives, it helps to look at both the positive and negative consequences of the change we want to create. For example, if I decide I want to change jobs and make more money, I can create a list of pros and cons to compare the advantages and disadvantages of the change I am considering.

PROS AND CONS OF CAREER CHANGE

+ Finding an interesting new job	− Accepting more responsibility
+ Making more money	− Leaving Friends

TAKING INITIATIVE

Reflection and planning get you to the starting line, but taking the initiative moves you forward. After graduating high school, I wasn't sure what I wanted to do with my life. I made a deal with my mom that if I found a good-paying job, I could defer college for a few years.

I was motivated and started working for AT&T/Pacific Bell when I was eighteen.

I found the job listing through an ad in our local paper. I showed up on the advertised date to take a test and be interviewed. As I walked into the office, they led me to a room where twenty other young ladies were sitting. We were all given a test with one hour to complete it. At the end, we waited while, one by one, each person's name was called. Each person was escorted into another office where they learned the results of their test and were interviewed.

I was sitting next to a young, redheaded girl. I asked her, "How do you think you did?"

She said, "I'm not sure. It looks like a lot of college graduates are here today, and they are all older than we are. My name is Bonnie."

I said, "Yeah." and I told her about the deal I had made with my mom. "Looks like I may be going straight to college," I said.

As the afternoon wore on, each person went into the small room for their meeting and then left. I was starting to believe that my mom was right; I needed to go to college. There we were, Bonnie and I, the last two, waiting for our results, feeling less and less confident about our chances of getting a job.

When I was called into the office, the woman doing the interviews said, "Congratulations! You did very well on your test. Tell me about yourself." I was so relieved. I didn't know what to say, but I shared where I lived and that I would like to have a job to get some work experience.

In a very professional way, she said, "We are starting a new clerical training program in Sacramento next week. Do you think you could start then?"

"Of course," I said, not realizing that I would need a car, which I didn't have.

When I got home, I told my mom, "I got a job. I have been hired for a clerical position with Pacific Bell, and I start next week. Can you help me buy a car?"

My mom was happy for me, and she said, "That's great! You can start paying rent for your bedroom."

"Really???" I said.

I continued to expand my professional experiences, and because of affirmative action, I had many opportunities to work in nontraditional roles. I spent time in the field as a construction manager and worked in engineering, creating blueprints for telephone facilities in new subdivisions.

After AT&T was split, each "Baby Bell" needed to develop its own strategic plan. I participated in this process, working with a management team to define the future of Pacific Bell. This was a difficult task because there were so many unknowns. We knew we couldn't hold on to the past and the way things had been before the split. And we would no longer have AT&T to bail us out if we did not meet our revenue projections at the end of the year. But while it was challenging, it was a great opportunity to learn about effectively managing change.

A RED SUIT IN A BLUE SUIT WORLD

Navigating change is an ongoing process. Our personal and work lives are constantly in flux. Having a clear purpose and understanding of what you want and where you want to go (even if the details are fuzzy) sets you on the right course.

After several years in management, I was selected to be assessed for executive-level positions, which involved participating in a Management Assessment Program (MAP). The evaluation brought up all my self-limiting beliefs about not being smart enough, but I gave it all I had.

Weeks later, I sat with an assessor from the program who reviewed my MAP results with me. He was very positive. However, one thing he said has stayed with me to this day. He said, "Barbara, you are a red suit in a blue suit world." When I heard this, my mind went immediately to my old beliefs: "I am different. I am not going to fit in." But I've learned a lot since then and now realize that being the "red suit" in the room is a role and a presence that can create great value and is one that I embrace.

Several months after my MAP assessment, I had a big change to consider. One that required me to reconsider my purpose. Pacific Bell began offering early retirement packages to their more senior employees. While I was only thirty-eight years old, I was within two weeks of eligibility. Jim had more years of service with Pacific Bell, and it was clear he was going to leave and start the next chapter of his life.

When I realized I was eligible, I became very conflicted. The part of me that loved change and adventure was excited about the possibility of retiring. The responsible side of me felt that I needed to stay and continue to advance my career and contribute a great paycheck to our family.

That night, I decided to tell Jim that I wanted to take the retirement package and leave the company. My heart was pounding. I felt as guilty as if I was about to tell him I was having an affair, which, of course, I was not. I was afraid of how he would respond to what I was proposing.

At dinner, I said, "There is something I need to share with you, and I want you to have an open mind."

When I told him what I was considering, he said, "I think we should take a vacation and discuss our options if you want to do this."

Soon after, we planned a week in Hawaii, where we could relax and talk. At the end of the week, we agreed that, at our ages, we had many ways to move forward to create our next chapter and generate income.

On the last afternoon of our trip, we were having lunch in Lahaina. We noticed a buzz in the restaurant, and we could hear people talking anxiously. We asked the waiter what all the commotion was about. She said, "Didn't you hear? The stock market just collapsed." This was Black Friday in October 1987. I felt as though the prize ticket I was holding — the ticket that would allow me to begin a new chapter of my life — had just been canceled.

We returned to work, and I decided I would still leave at the end of the year when Jim retired. We would both start our next chapters. When I made the announcement at work, it was not received very positively by the senior management team. They said, "This was not the plan that we had for you. There will be many new management positions and opportunities." However, I was clear that I was done with feasibility studies, new product launches, and quarterly revenue projections. I was ready for something new.

I was so excited about the freedom I would have to design my future. But soon after walking out the door at the end of that year, the realization of the decision I had made set in, and it began to feel like a weight. I was unemployed, with no clear idea about what I wanted to do.

As I thought about the many experiences I'd had in my career, the idea of becoming a coach and working with new technology companies came to me. I knew it would be challenging because, at that time, there really weren't any professional coaches. I was not sure how I was going to convince people to hire me as a business coach, but I was ready to get started.

I went to Silicon Valley, prepared to be a red suit in the new technology revolution, and the timing was right. Thirty-plus years later, I'm still coaching, and the field of professional coaching is the fastest-growing industry in the world, with an average yearly growth of 67 percent and an estimated 4.4 million coaches globally.[7]

As I have shared, it takes courage and commitment to create change in your life. There must be a compelling reason. I always ask my clients, "What is your purpose for making this change?" You have to know your purpose.

A GOAL WITHOUT A PURPOSE IS POINTLESS

It is great to set goals, but a goal that is not grounded in your personal purpose and the vision you have for your life will ultimately become hard to achieve. Passion and a commitment to something greater than the goal are needed in order to maintain the motivation to achieve it.

Too many times, I see people declare a goal without getting clear about why they have the goal. As I interview new clients and ask them, "What do you want?" I might hear, "I want a better relationship with my partner."

I then ask the question, "Why do you want a better relationship with your partner?"

A GOAL THAT IS NOT GROUNDED IN YOUR PERSONAL PURPOSE AND THE VISION YOU HAVE FOR YOUR LIFE WILL ULTIMATELY BECOME HARD TO ACHIEVE.

And I hear something like, "I am tired of not being a priority for them."

To this, I will say, "That is what you *don't* want. What *do* you want in a better relationship?"

This is when many people stop and think for a few minutes, considering what it is that they really *do* want. After a while, they might say, "I want more time together," or "I would like better communication." Whatever their answer, *this* is the real purpose of the goal.

I have learned that what people say they want from coaching in the beginning is rarely what they really want. There is always something deeper. Being curious and asking questions eventually leads to the real purpose of their goal. Once discovered, this is the motivation that will keep them committed to the coaching relationship. If they have a vision of what they will experience when they have achieved their goal, they are more likely to achieve it.

Present State to Desired State

The desire for change occurs when we take the time to evaluate where we are in our lives. This is the current state that we find ourselves in, and perhaps it doesn't feel quite right. It could be a relationship that isn't working, an unfilled career, a lack of security (either financially or personally), health concerns, or unfulfilled dreams.

When working with clients, I spend a significant amount of time trying to better understand their present state (where they are in their lives) and what they want in their future. I help them get clear about exactly what it is that they want and what that means to them. I help them imagine how their life will be different when they have achieved the desired change.

Whether their goal is more confidence, better relationships, improved communication, or a change in their environment, as we work together, we can begin to identify the resources they need in order to move toward the change they want in their life.

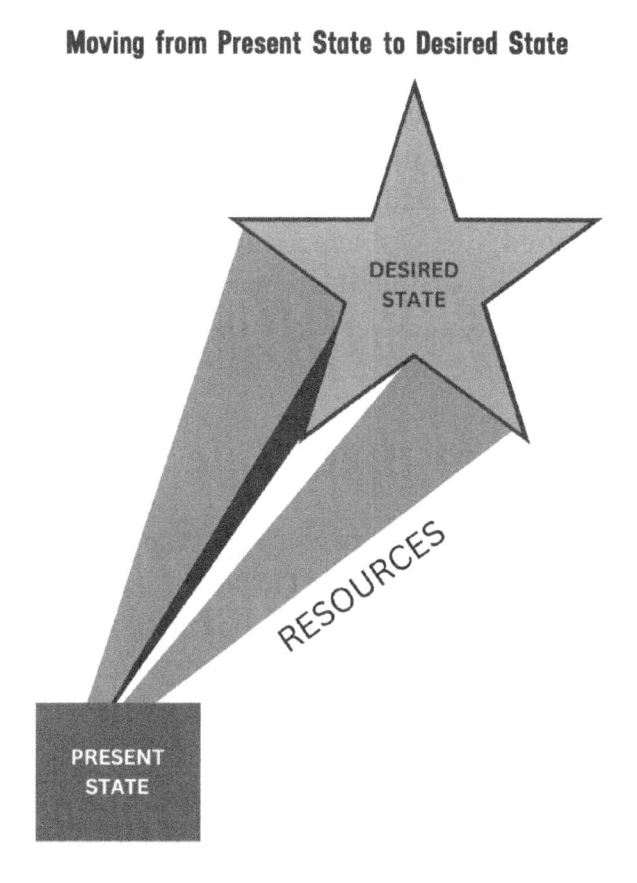

Moving from Present State to Desired State

I once worked with a wonderful, loving woman who had been overweight for years. She had tried many times to lose weight, and the weight always came back. She wanted to move from her present state of being overweight and feeling unhealthy to a new state that would change how she experienced her life. I asked her why she wanted to lose weight, and she said, "To be healthier."

Rather than making my assumption about why she wanted to be healthier, I asked, "Why do you want to be healthy?"

She thought for a minute and then said, "So that I can live longer, spend time with my grandchildren, and have the energy to play with them."

I said, "Then that is your goal — to develop a healthy lifestyle that will enable you to have a long life and lots of energy so you can enjoy time with your grandchildren."

We began to focus on what her desired state would look like. What would she be doing? How would she feel about her health? As she described her future state in detail, I could see and hear the excitement she was feeling about her future.

As the weeks passed, we began to identify the resources she would need in order to get to the future that she wanted. She created a plan that included eating a healthy diet and exercising regularly. She enrolled her family to support her new eating practices. She began making time for meditation to keep herself focused on the vision of herself living a healthy life and playing with her grandchildren.

I recently saw a social media post from her. She had shared a picture from her granddaughter's high school graduation. As I saw them standing together, it made me smile, knowing she had achieved her goal and realized her vision for her life.

YOUR NEXT CHAPTER

> **When Thinking About Designing the Next Chapter of Your Life, Consider the Following Questions:**
>
> - What new opportunities do you want to explore?
> - What natural talents and capabilities do you have?
> - How do you want your life to be different?
> - What risks are you willing to take?
> - What resources and support will you need?

Once you have answered these questions and begun to feel a spark of excitement, the only thing needed is to declare your purpose. With a clear purpose, you can truly begin to envision how your life could be.

Then, and only then, you can create goals for yourself that will move you forward. Goals are merely milestones — the steps you need to take to achieve your vision. Have faith and trust yourself. Stay focused on your vision, and your goals will empower you to achieve it.

EMPOWERING BEHAVIORS

- Empower yourself to see what you want.
- Empower yourself to choose what you want.
- Empower yourself to declare what you want.
- Empower yourself to acknowledge your feelings.
- Empower yourself to request what you want instead of waiting.

Over the years, I have helped hundreds of clients work through this empowering behaviors process. It is always wonderful to hear from them years later after they have realized their vision. The empowerment coaching helped them shift perspectives and see what was possible for them. If you can envision it, you can create it!

PART 2

COMMIT TO TAKING ACTION

ROAM IF YOU WANT TO, ROAM AROUND THE WORLD.

—THE B-52S

CHAPTER 4

NO BACK DOORS

*O*nce you set your purpose, decisions and choices become more straightforward. You are working within a clearly defined vision. There are always choices in life. While you may not like all the choices you have, you can make ones that work for you. A clear purpose keeps you moving in a desired direction. It keeps you on course and helps you resist the feeling that it would be easier to find a way out. No back doors!

I began working with Dan when he was a young, twenty-four-year-old account executive in a public relations and marketing firm. The purpose of our coaching was to help him lead account teams more effectively. I continued working with him throughout his career as he advanced to become the global managing director for consumer accounts with Fleishman Hillard, one of the largest public relations and marketing firms in the world.

Five years ago, Dan had reached a turning point in his career. He knew he had to make a decision about his future. While he was very successful and highly regarded for the work he was doing, he was debating whether to stay with

Fleishman Hillard or take off on his own. He told me that the words from the song "Roam" from the B-52s kept playing over and over in his head. Throughout our years of coaching, he had often talked about his love for food and had even volunteered to assist a small restaurant business in San Francisco by helping to improve its marketing strategies and develop its brand.

In December 2018, as the time for Dan to decide was approaching, I invited him to my place in Sonoma County to work with him on his future plans. Once he arrived, I told him that I wanted to take him through an experiential process. He would need to let go of his brain and just center himself on the experience and the moment. I asked Dan to stand in the middle of my office and close his eyes. I said that I wanted him to imagine how his life would be three years in the future. I then said, "Tell me what you see. Describe it in detail."

Each time he started talking from his head, I coached him to get in touch with his experience. I asked him to see his future and describe it without any filters or judgment about what he was saying. As he connected more deeply to his experience, he said, "I am in a room with other people standing around a large, high-top white table. The people around me are talking about consumer trends, analyzing the texture of packaging materials, and reviewing competitors' websites. Other people are laying out products for a taste test. Everyone is touching and tasting things, and we're all sharing ideas and enthusiasm about our common goal." When Dan left, he was excited about exploring the option of working with and creating food products.

After much thought and consideration, Dan decided to pursue his dream of creating a business with food. As we talked about different options, he told me that his vision was to create an experience with food that was delicious, memorable, and brought people a feeling of joy.

With his years of experience as a brand manager and marketing communications executive, he knew he always had the option to work in-house at other companies. As we talked, there were days when he would vacillate back and forth on whether this was a good idea or if he could be successful working as an entrepreneur in a new arena. One day, I said, "Dan, if you move forward, there can be no back doors."

Forward, Not Back

The first thing I worked with Dan on was to identify his purpose for starting a food-based business. I told him, "Having a clear purpose is like the rudder on a boat. It will help guide you as you move forward."

Dan's purpose was "To create a product that was delicious and memorable, in a way that could be delivered to people across the country, bringing joy and excitement so that people could share the experience with others."

Once we had clearly defined Dan's purpose, we began to look at specific outcomes that would need to be achieved in order to make the business a success. The first thing Dan said he wanted was to find the right business partner. He had met a woman named Tarran who worked at Milk Bar, an award-winning bakery known for its desserts, and decided he wanted her to be the first person on the team. He said, "She has a very specialized talent and experience in what we will need to be able to do."

HAVING A CLEAR PURPOSE IS LIKE THE RUDDER ON A BOAT. IT WILL HELP GUIDE YOU AS YOU MOVE FORWARD.

Dan was concerned that he would not be able to persuade her to join his team. He said, "What if she doesn't want to come on board? If I can't get her, then I will need to start from scratch and engineer all the recipes myself."

Dan and I spent time brainstorming ways that he could convince Tarran to leave the secure and established position she had at Milk Bar and join him on this new venture. He thought they would make a great team. Dan felt that she might be open to it and be excited to have the opportunity to use her creativity. Dan approached Tarran with the same enthusiasm and excitement he had about starting this venture, and she agreed to join him.

By the early part of 2019, Dan had a solid business and financial plan to get his company, BlissBomb, started. His product was a box of delicious baked donuts that melted in your mouth. The flavors were exceptional, and they were decorated like little works of art. The donuts were shipped in a bright, colorful box that could be saved and used again.

Dan faced many challenges that first year while developing the recipes with Tarran and testing different flavors to create a baked (not fried) donut that would be truly unique. They tried different types of shipping to ensure each donut in the box stayed fresh and that the presentation of colors, glazes, and toppings would be intact when they arrived.

Dan left San Francisco, where he had lived for thirty years, and found a commercial kitchen in New York City. BlissBomb began producing donuts that could be shipped across the United States.

Later that year, I got a card from Dan that said, "I am standing in my vision." The picture that he had created almost two years earlier had come true. He wrote, "Today, I found myself standing in our commercial kitchen around a tall, white baking table. I was talking with Tarran about the donut recipes we are going to use and our packaging, marketing, and customers, and I realized this was the picture I had seen the day I was standing in your office."

"Yes!" I thought. "I am glad he realized that if you can envision it, you can create it."

It was early in spring 2020 when Dan launched his operations in New York City. Shortly after that, COVID hit, and Manhattan became like a ghost town. Fortunately, he had set up BlissBomb to be primarily e-commerce, so he was optimistic. He said, " Everyone is being sent home to work, and the ability to send treats anywhere in the country amid a collapsing world seems like a good idea."

Dan began approaching companies about sending gift boxes to their employees to help encourage them and keep their morale up during this crazy time. He thought that by July, the whole COVID thing would be over, and he would have established a great base of repeat customers.

Months later, as he was struggling to keep his new business going, I asked him, "Have you been thinking about prying open that back door a bit?"

He said, "You know, I guess I have been operating on autopilot. I haven't even thought once about just packing it up and heading back to San Francisco."

When companies started to send BlissBomb packages to their employees to help them feel connected, he knew he had made the right decision. He told me later, "I knew I had to test myself. For most of my career, someone else made the big, hard decisions about business operations while I focused on account management. COVID was an opportunity for me to take myself out of my comfort zone, and while that was terrifying, it has been rewarding at the same time.

Dan shared with me later, "This was a real opportunity to think about the well-being of my team before worrying about the bottom line. For BlissBomb, it worked. I plan to approach all big decisions this way going forward. I expect we'll continue to see it manifest what's best for the company."

USING THE 3 PS: PURPOSE, PRODUCTS, PROCESS

Most of us organize and focus our days based on what we are going to do rather than how we want our day to be. This is a key distinction. To shift toward a "how I want my day to be" mindset, I apply a purpose, products, and process (3Ps) approach. It is a powerful planning and thinking tool that can be used for coordinating an executive retreat, organizing a vacation, or even setting up a dinner party.

I actually wake up every day and imagine how I want it to be. What will be my **purpose** for the day? Purpose isn't objective; it is subjective. I might say to myself, "I want today to be fun!" From there, I begin to think of things I might do that would be fun for me, like gardening, writing, or being with friends. This sense of purpose is what I meant when I shared with Dan how a clear purpose was like the rudder on a boat guiding your way.

Once I have identified my purpose for the day, I think about what outcomes or **products** I want to achieve. Some days, my purpose is focused on writing. I ask myself, "Okay, how much do I want to write today?" Then, I can quantify the outcomes I want for the day. Lastly, I plan my day. I determine when I will write, how long I will write, and what resources I might need. This is the **process** I use. By spending time at the beginning of the day to gain clarity, I am now better equipped to succeed.

This does not mean that all days go perfectly. However, by creating a plan, even if it is just in your mind, you'll know where and when you can make adjustments if necessary. I have used the 3P model with my clients for thirty years, and they have found it to be one of the most valuable planning tools they have used.

3P'S

- **Purpose** – Why are you doing this? (subjective)
- **Products** or outcomes – What will you create or produce? (objective)
- **Process** – What are the steps or actions you will take to fulfill the purpose and achieve your desired products/outcomes?

GETTING OUT OF YOUR COMFORT ZONE

As Dan recognized, he would need to get out of his comfort zone if BlissBomb was going to survive. A comfort zone is like a warm bath of water we enjoy being in. The temperature is just right — not too hot, not too cold.

Being in our comfort zone is familiar. While it's not always completely comfortable, we know what to expect. As shown in the comfort zone figure, it is shaped by beliefs formed from past experiences. The attitudes, frame of mind, and assumptions we make have evolved from previous experiences, and these dictate what we think is or is not possible. Our comfort zone influences the choices and actions we take.

A point I often make when working with clients is that "Change cannot occur when you are comfortable." Staying in our comfort zone results in us doing the same thing and creating the same outcomes. By stretching and getting outside our comfort zone, we are then able to see new possibilities and create new experiences.

Comfort Zone

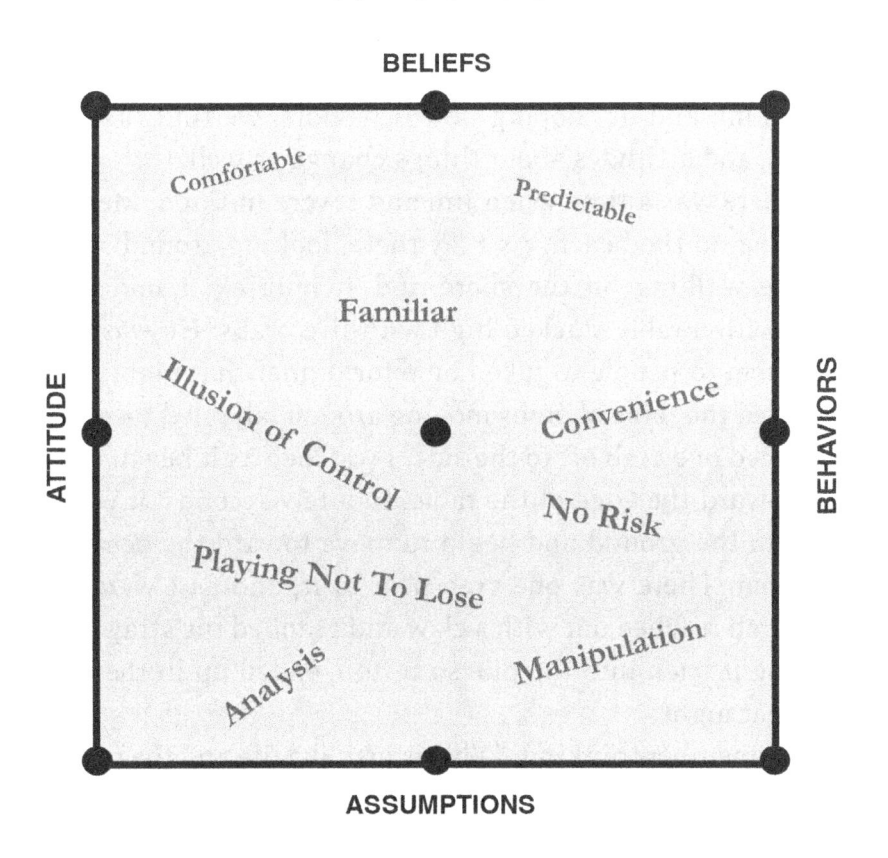

BELIEFS

ATTITUDE — BEHAVIORS

Comfortable
Predictable
Familiar
Illusion of Control
Convenience
No Risk
Playing Not To Lose
Analysis
Manipulation

ASSUMPTIONS

In order to create change in your life, you must be willing to leave your comfort zone. In my coaching experience, this is the hardest thing for people to accept. They want to create something new, but they also want to stay where they are comfortable.

When we stretch ourselves, we begin to see how much more we are capable of — once we get past the initial discomfort. I love when clients come back to me and say, "That was really exciting. I didn't think I could do it."

Holding on to our comfort zone gives us a false sense of security and control. It prevents us from taking risks and pushing ourselves. I remind my clients that once they push themselves a little bit by developing new practices or skills, they will never go back to the way they were before. By stretching and developing new behaviors, we find that our beliefs and attitudes about things change as well.

There was a time when Jim and I were in Cabo, Mexico, relaxing on the beach. As I lay there, looking around at the people walking on the shore and swimming, I noticed a man with a table stacked high with live crabs. He was selling them to people to take home for dinner that night. As I watched the table of crabs moving around, all piled together, I noticed one crab off to the side. I watched as it began moving toward the edge of the table. In a few seconds, it would drop to the ground and begin to move toward the ocean to freedom. There was one crab next to it, and as I watched, that crab reached out with a claw and grabbed the stray crab, pulling it back into the pile so it, too, ended up in the crab pot that night.

I remember thinking, "This is just like life and the people I work with." So many times, I have heard clients share, "I

HOLDING ON TO OUR COMFORT ZONE GIVES US A FALSE SENSE OF SECURITY AND CONTROL.

just don't know how to start something new. My wife thinks I am crazy, and my friends don't want me to move. How do I know if I am making the right decision?"

Often, when we go through changes in our lives, there are people around us who don't want us to change. Because we are all interconnected in so many ways, people become fearful when someone they care about decides to make big changes in their lives and move on. At some level, they know that it will affect the relationship and perhaps require that they change also.

I have seen this many times in relationships. One person will want to make a change — perhaps go back to school or get a job or even decide it would be a good idea to sell their house and move. The partner in the relationship will be impacted by this and may not agree or support the change.

Perhaps they fear that they are losing them or that they won't be able to spend as much time with them in the way that they always have. This can create tension in the relationship.

It is necessary to consider the other people involved in your life who will be impacted by your decisions to make changes. I suggest being very honest with them about what you are considering and being open to receiving their input as a way to include them in the process. It is so much better to have them in alignment than to try to take on a big change without the support and resources you have around you.

DO WHAT IS DIFFICULT FIRST

There is an old saying, "If the first thing you do each morning is to eat a live frog, you can go through the day with the satisfaction of knowing that is probably the worst thing that is going to happen to you all day long!"

Productivity and time management coach Brian Tracy uses this quote in his book *Eat That Frog!*[8] He suggests that we are fully capable of selecting our most important task at a particular moment, starting that task, and completing the task, both quickly and well. Following these steps will probably have a greater impact on your success than any other quality or skill you can develop.

It's an interesting concept. In my experience, my most important tasks are pretty big. I feel that if I start with the big tasks, then very little else would get checked off my list for the day. Instead, I often decide to procrastinate by knocking out several smaller tasks quickly, knowing that the one big task would consume much of my time. Could "eating the frog" really increase my productivity? Could I really get more done in less time — including the things that are most important to me? And would this actually result in less stress?

So, practical me thought, "Let's test this out." I had several tasks ranked as important and additional tasks I believed were challenging (aka outside my comfort zone).

Test Day 1: With a big gulp, just as I imagined I would do when eating a real frog, I stepped into a task that needed to be done that day — one I had been procrastinating about doing. I had found my FROG! Two and one-half hours later, it was complete. Because finishing it was so incredibly energizing, I took on my next task and still got to many of the less important items on my list. I was amazed.

Test Day 2: With the positive results from day one, I continued this test into day two and had similar success. Starting with the biggest task quickly became my daily practice. My gulps were getting easier, and the frogs were getting tastier. Brian Tracy adds, "If you have to eat two frogs, eat the ugliest one first!" This means if you have more than one important task to complete, begin with the most important or most difficult task first. Start the task immediately, and don't stop or move on to anything else until the task is done.

As a proud multitasker, it was an additional challenge for me to persist until the task was complete. But clearly, this was what allowed me to get my first frog eaten in two and one-half hours versus over the course of an entire day, saving me from a day full of stress and constantly telling myself that I had to get this task done. One final quote from Brian, "If you have to eat a live frog, it does not pay to sit and look at it for a very long time!" Wise words.

Stay True to Yourself

When I decided to sell our house and move to a smaller property, I heard from many people who said, "You will regret this. You will never find another home like this one. It will kill Jim." I knew the decision I made was the right one, even if people around me didn't agree. As I was growing up and trying to be like all the other kids, I remember my dad saying to me, "To thy own self be true."

As I prepared for our move, I kept reminding myself that this was a good decision. It would benefit both Jim and me. I would feel less stressed, and I would be able to spend more time with Jim. As it turned out, once we were settled into our new house and people came to visit, they would tell me, "This is perfect. You made the right choice."

Staying true to our own beliefs, doing the hard things first, and getting outside of our comfort zones are not easy. It requires having a clear purpose and trusting ourselves. When combined, these behaviors help you move forward and change. That's what got me through the move and helped me arrive at a new place in my life — all at the same time.

CREATING A POWERFUL PURPOSE AND CLEAR VISION WILL GET YOU WHERE YOU WANT TO GO.

CHAPTER 5

CLARITY OF PURPOSE

When guided by a clear purpose and vision, we are able to set a solid course for our lives. Many times, we don't spend enough time defining our purpose before beginning something new. Instead, we react to a change in the moment.

With a lack of clarity, it's easy to constantly look back and doubt our actions. In some cases, it shows a lack of trust in ourselves and our ability to create what we want. Having a clear purpose to guide us and knowing what we want to create changes things. It's like setting sail and staying focused on the horizon.

When I was working in the corporate world, so much energy was placed on people's positions or power and authority. I was even guilty of this at times. As the product manager for a product generating 350 million dollars annually, I had the authority to make decisions about marketing campaigns, product launches, and sales strategies to ensure the product's forecasted revenue was achieved.

When the revenue results didn't reflect the forecast, it was easy to start playing the blame game. When guided by ego instead of purpose, we will do and say almost anything to keep from looking bad. To protect our egos, we behave the way that we want people to see us (i.e., in charge, in control, confident, with authority, etc.). When our results aren't what we want, we often look to blame others instead of taking responsibility and looking for what we could have done differently. This limits the ability to identify what changes could be made to create different results.

As mentioned, I often ask clients, "What is your purpose? Why are you doing this?" My favorite follow-up question takes it further, "If you achieve this change, how will your life be different?" When guided by your purpose instead of your ego, there is something at stake that is more important than how you look to others. We must let go of our ego and do whatever it takes to fulfill our purpose.

My purpose as a product manager was to create a high-quality product for our consumers that provided satisfaction, reduced their expenses, and also brought valuable revenue to the organization. My focus was on looking for efficiencies in product design to reduce costs so that savings could be passed on to the customer. This needed to be accomplished while still providing a product that was valuable and that sales teams could market. And all of this had to be done while increasing revenue for the company.

If those goals were not achieved, I would first look at the decisions I had made and the results to see what needed to change. Always looking at ourselves first is where the learning occurs. It is easy to point fingers. It is harder to look at our own actions and decisions to try to find solutions. But by

WE MUST LET GO OF OUR EGO AND DO WHATEVER IT TAKES TO FULFILL OUR PURPOSE.

taking individual responsibility — owning both your wins and losses — and fine-tuning your purpose, you are more likely to have success in the future.

GETTING CLEAR ON YOUR PURPOSE

Establishing an individual purpose is important, but we're often working with others. In group situations, it's equally important to have a clear, agreed-upon purpose. It helps for all parties to work toward the same goal. I encountered the importance of this firsthand when working as a facilitator at a parent seminar.

Mary's teenage daughter Pamela was headed for trouble. At the age of fourteen, a girl who had once been a very respectful teenager and loved spending time with her parents had turned into someone Mary barely recognized. The harder Mary tried to reach her, the more Pamela withdrew.

There was little communication, and when Mary did try to talk to Pamela, she usually heard "F... you!" as a response. Mary found that Pamela had been lying about a number of things, like who she was with when she went out, what she was doing, and why she was not coming home at the agreed-upon time. Mary knew things had reached a critical point when, at age fifteen, Pamela took her dad's seven-inch buck knife from his dresser, stole the family car, and, with no driving experience, disappeared.

It was clear that Pamela needed help. There were court dates, therapist meetings, legal fees, and penalties to pay. One day, a close friend who'd had similar challenges with his teenager years before said to Mary, "I know this is really hard on you. Perhaps you and John should look into the residential school I sent my son to."

Mary cried, "I could never do that."

Both worked for airlines and traveled regularly for work (John was a pilot, and Mary was a long-time flight attendant). While they were gone, they found themselves constantly consumed with worry about their daughter. They knew they had to create change in Pamela's behavior, so Mary and John had to make one of the hardest decisions of their life.

Eventually, they decided the best thing for Pamela would be to place her in a residential school. There, she would continue her education and work with other teens to regain self-respect and an understanding of the responsible behavior necessary to lead a whole and healthy life.

One weekend, they took Pamela for a drive, saying they were going camping, packing clothes, pillows, and sleeping bags — a necessary lie to get her in the car. As they arrived at the school, Mary got out of the car and opened the door for Pamela. She said, crying, "This is the hardest thing I have ever done, and I love you so much."

Pamela looked around, confused, and asked, "Where are we?"

Mary replied, "You are going to be staying here for the next year. You, your dad, and I are going to be working on how to improve our communication and make changes in the way we do things as a family going forward."

"Oh F.... no!" Pamela screamed. "You and Dad are just going to fly away and leave me here like you always do."

For Mary's daughter, this felt not only like punishment but also abandonment. In some ways, it felt the same for Mary. She had doubts about whether she had done the right thing.

The school helped coach parents of the teens on ways to support their child and how to create a healthy home environment for their child to come home to. Mary and John attended seminars with other parents and found comfort in knowing that many of them had shared similar experiences.

I was a facilitator at one of the seminars where I met Mary and John. In my first lecture, I asked the group, "Do you have a family purpose?" They all looked at me with blank stares, trying to figure out what to say.

One woman said, "We love each other."

I said, "Of course! That's why all of you are here." I explained that a family purpose was a statement that described how they wanted to be as a family. Just like in an organization or business, families should have a purpose/mission statement that describes what they intend to create.

By now, the parents seemed to be more relaxed, and I could see that they were actively paying attention. I drew a pyramid on the easel that showed how purpose was the foundation — the thing that helps us to create a vision for the future. Goals are the milestones that keep us on track and measure how we are moving toward our vision and fulfilling our purpose. The action is the least important part of the pyramid, although most of us spend more time thinking about what we need to do instead of asking ourselves, "What is my purpose?" "Why am I doing this?"

Purpose Pyramid

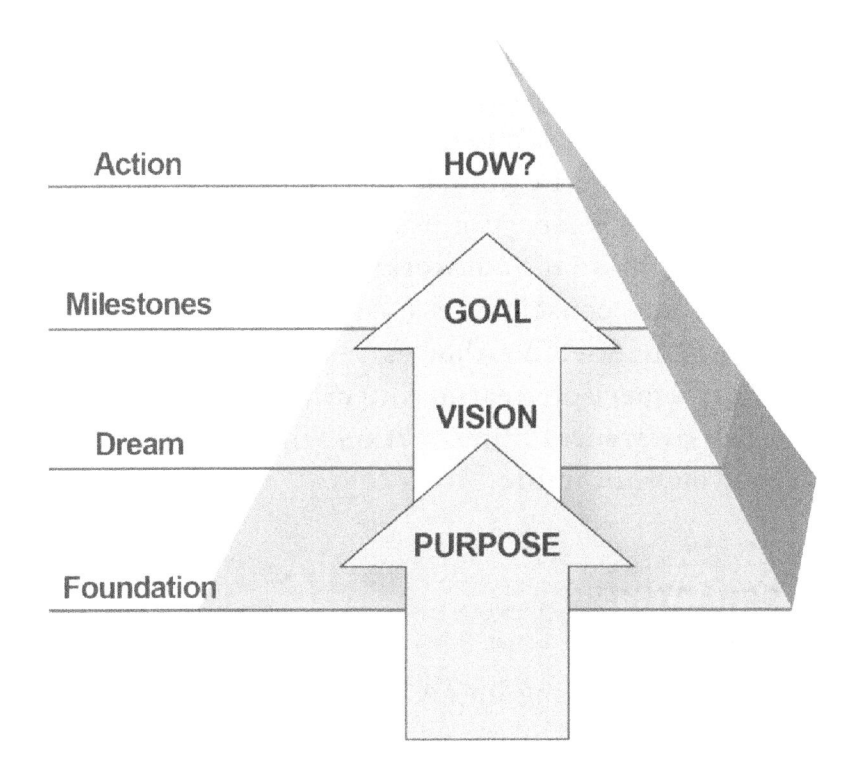

```
Action       HOW?
Milestones   GOAL
             VISION
Dream
             PURPOSE
Foundation
```

As I worked with the parents that weekend, they began to develop a clear purpose for their family and their intention for their child with the residential school.

I asked them, "What is your vision? What do you want to see in the future for your family?"

They expressed their family purposes in individual ways, but the sentiments were similar. Their vision was to have their child come home and go on to live a whole and healthy adult life. They wanted their family to share a clear purpose and values that they would all live by.

Get In the Driver's Seat of Your Life

Living life with purpose means being truly willing to examine ourselves and understand what makes us tick. It embraces principles that support being in the driver's seat of our own lives. When I accept that everything happens for a reason, I can look for the lesson and take responsibility for my part in it. If I am willing to examine and learn from what's not working, I increase my awareness level and consciousness. This, in turn, allows me to make more effective choices based on my purpose. A necessary aspect of creating intention is committed action. Self-awareness minus action will never create the change you want in life.

BE PROACTIVE

In 1989, I was setting up my coaching practice and had the opportunity to work with Dr. Stephen Covey. His work has continued to inspire my coaching, and through the years, I have recommended applying his principles to countless clients. His book, *The Seven Habits of Highly Effective People,* has sold over 40 million copies and has been translated into fifty languages worldwide. His first habit, "Be Proactive," talks about taking action rather than being reactive.[9]

Years ago, my youngest sister, a mother of three, was overwhelmed by the increasing costs of her growing family. One day on the phone, she shared, "I just don't know how we are going to get ahead of all these expenses."

SELF-AWARENESS MINUS ACTION WILL NEVER CREATE THE CHANGE YOU WANT IN LIFE.

I could hear that she was reacting to her situation, and I asked her, "What is one thing that you could do to begin to feel like you are making progress?"

She thought for a moment and then said, "Maybe I could call the bank and ask them about a bill consolidation loan."

I said, "Well, it is worth a try. And if that doesn't work out, maybe they can give you some useful advice on what to do."

A few days later, she called me and shared, "The bank has been very helpful. We are consolidating all the larger bills into one loan, and we have created a calendar and a plan to pay down the rest."

As the months passed, I would check in on how she was doing. Each time we spoke, she shared how much creating their plan had helped her feel more empowered to make the decisions needed to manage their budget. She had learned an important lesson about being proactive versus reactive.

Proactive Time Management

The same is true when learning the discipline of time management. Dr. Covey cited a great example in his book, what he calls the production/production capabilities balance (or P/PC balance). Essentially, this means people and organizations can improve production by investing in production capabilities. Too often, people and organizations expect production to increase without making the needed investment in training, new practices, new systems, etc.

Similarly, in coaching, I remind clients to invest in ways they can become more productive or effective in their lives. Too often, organizations spend time focused on expecting people to produce at higher and higher rates of performance.

However, they don't invest in training or self-empowerment programs designed to increase employees' capabilities because they fear it will be too costly.

In coaching sessions, I've found that two things limit people's ability to manage time effectively. The first is not having clear priorities and an understanding of what is most important. The second is not having the discipline to say no to people who want to use their time unnecessarily. Hundreds of hours are spent each year having people attend meetings that they do not need to be involved in or meetings that are poorly planned and inefficient — both resulting in hours of wasted time.

Each week, I ask myself what my priorities are and then schedule them on my calendar. Each day, I make a list of at least six things that I will accomplish that day. If, at the end of the day, I haven't finished my list, I add those incomplete items to the top of my list for the next day. By having this list and scheduling my time, I sometimes must say no to things that come up that will prevent me from keeping the agreement I have made with myself for the day. Of course, if there is something urgent or a crisis, I will make whatever changes are necessary. It is critical to know what is actually important to accomplish so that you do not spend your day reacting to others or to situations that are not critical.

I have used this practice for years. One of the things you learn when you are self-employed is that "If it is to be, it is up to me." By making a to-do list based on priorities, you take the first step toward accomplishing something for the day. I am a big believer in incentives. Once I have tackled my first big priority, I give myself a reward. Maybe it's getting in the car and going to Starbucks to get my favorite coffee or going out to my garden for a walk to enjoy the weather — simple things that also break up the day.

VALUES - THE KEY TO YOUR FRONT DOOR

A key component of the work that I did in the seminars with the teens' parents was to have them evaluate their family values. I explained to them that while many people talk about values, few actually live their values day to day. We talk about the value of personal integrity, but we sometimes avoid telling the truth. We show up late, don't keep our agreements, or make excuses.

When working with the parents, I drew a picture of a house on the easel and said, "Values are the keys to your front door. You need to know your family values and talk about how you will live them." I explained how every member of the family is responsible for living aligned with the family values. I went on to tell them that I understood that teenagers test everything — especially family values. But, a lack of clear values and boundaries contributed to the chaos they were experiencing with their teens. And while it was hard to hear, they seemed to recognize that this was true. In order for a family to work and thrive, every member needs to live within their values system in order to earn and keep their key to the door.

I also asked the parents to imagine an emergency that required them to leave their home quickly with only a moment's notice, leaving them time to grab five things to take with them. This had actually happened to Jim and I. After our fire scare in Sonoma, I thought about the things I had taken from our home and why I had picked those things. I discovered it was because they represented our values.

As the parents discussed what they would take, I listed the items on the easel. One man shared that he would take his softball mitt.

When I asked why, he replied, "Because it reminds me of when I was younger and would play catch with my dad when he came home from work."

"So," I said, "it represents having fun together as a family?"

"Yes," he responded, "and we have fun in a lot of other ways too."

As the list grew from softball mitt to computers, jewelry, pictures, and financial records, we discussed how each item represented a core value for the individual who added it. Creating this list of values was necessary to create the change needed to help heal the family.

I told the parents, "You will need to share these values with your teen and other family members to create alignment." Having this alignment is the critical first step for making changes in the home environment so that values can be demonstrated and respected by all family members each day.

At the end of the three-day seminar, the parents had written their purpose and established clear values for their family. They committed to taking on the responsibility of using the valuable tools they had been given. I shared with them that this would require a great deal of work on their part and that their commitment would be tested. However, if they did the work and applied the tools, they had a better than 50 percent chance of realizing their vision for their family.

Mary and John stayed the course. They developed their family purpose and values and worked with their daughter

Pamela so she understood them. She agreed to live her life aligned with the family values they had created. When it was time for Pamela to come home, Mary asked me, "What if I can't do this? It has been so much work, and we really want our family to be happy together again. I am so scared things won't be any different."

I told Mary, "You need to trust yourself. You, John, and Pamela have worked hard together to get to this place. It was tough at times, but you have created the tools for your family to move forward."

It has been several years since Pamela returned home. Yes, they did have some rough times, but they all got through it together. Today, Pamela is a professional sales representative making six figures and a mother of four. She is starting to face her own challenges with her teenage daughters. Pamela and Mary can now laugh instead of being afraid because they have the tools that they learned years ago and know just what to do to create trust and honest communication in the family.

Alignment with Values

When you find yourself in a difficult situation that is not in alignment with your values, you can actually feel the discomfort in your body. When this happens, it takes courage to let people know they have crossed your boundaries. While not always easy, speaking up is the best way to get people to respect you and what you stand for.

Years ago, when I was young, I worked in a construction environment where the majority of my coworkers were men. There were many times when the conversations

I heard made me very uncomfortable. As a young professional woman, I was afraid to say anything, but I can still remember the discomfort I felt. Today, I wouldn't hesitate to let people know my thoughts, but I had to earn and learn this confidence. To my younger self and those struggling to find their voice: "Stay in alignment with your values, and you can do it!"

When reflecting on the part that values play in making choices, I believe that none of us can truly know what our values are unless we take the time to review the results we are creating in our lives. It is very empowering when we are able to see the evidence of our values. Values are the guiding principles by which we choose to live our lives. They are individually chosen and based on our beliefs and life experiences. Families and organizations that have aligned values have a higher degree of integrity and harmony in their environment. When your values are clear, it is easier to make choices that will support them.

Having clarity about your personal purpose, career purpose, and family purpose will always assist you in making the right decisions when it comes to creating change. Combining these with your personal values will help you look to your future and see if the change is right for you.

I often work with clients to help them manage career changes. We always discuss the purpose for making the change and what they want from their new job. By clarifying their purpose and values, they can then determine whether a job is right for them. Knowing your purpose and values makes it easier to know when to say yes and when to say no.

STEPS TO SETTING INTENTION

Building the Bridge as You Walk on It, by Robert E. Quinn, is a wonderful book that talks about how we can create change around us through the power of our own intention.[10] Too often, we wait to start a new chapter in our lives until we feel that we have all the answers or are forced to change because of a crisis, either personal or professional.

I always remember the scene in *Indiana Jones – The Last Crusade* where Harrison Ford's character was trying to escape a dangerous situation, and he found himself standing on a ledge on the side of a mountain with a big drop-off and nowhere to run. Then he heard the voice of his father telling him to trust that if he stepped out, a bridge would appear. It took him a great deal of courage and a leap of faith to overcome his fear of falling, but he trusted the voice and wisdom of his father and did what he was told. As he stepped off the ledge, a bridge appeared, and he escaped to safety.

The following steps are meant to serve as a guide so you can confidently build your bridge as you walk it.

Step 1: Set Your Purpose

Get clear about your day right at the start. Take five minutes to reflect on how you want your day to be. How do you want to feel at the end of the day? What is your vision of success? How will you be in relationship with others? What is the experience you intend to create? Allow yourself to become empowered and feel confident about the adventure the day can bring. Focus on positive intentions, not what you might be avoiding.

Step 2: Decide What You Want to Create Today

Review your priorities for the day. Be sure to include yourself as a priority, and schedule some time to practice self-care. Allow yourself some space between activities to minimize time conflicts and to keep from getting behind. Look at each part of your day as a separate chunk of time that has a specific desired outcome. If you do this, you will be able to step into each event or engagement with a purpose and end up with the outcomes you want. It is like sorting the laundry before you start to wash your clothes. To get the best results, set up priorities for your day.

Step 3: Determine How You Will Know if You've Succeeded

How will you know that you have accomplished your intention? What outcomes will you expect when achieving your intention? Some examples include, "I will feel less stress." "I will have participated in a meeting and provided collaboration and teamwork." "I will have learned something new about the project I am working on." "I will have had the time I want with my family today."

Step 4: Do an End-of-Day Reflection/Check-In

Take a few minutes at the end of your day to check in with yourself. How did the day go? How did it mirror your morning intention? Challenge yourself to look at your day from a neutral place. First, look at all of the things that you accomplished. For those areas where you saw some changes — what were they? Look at the attitude that you held, your communication, and how you managed your time to support your intention. Then, let it ALL go. Lastly, acknowledge yourself for being willing to build the bridge as you walk it and get a good night's sleep. Tomorrow is a new day!

Knowing Your Why

The steps required to create change begin with a clear purpose — knowing your "why." You should be able to answer the question, "Why is this change important to me?" It sets your purpose, which is the foundation of anything you create in life. If you don't know why you are making the change, then you will become confused as you move forward, looking at all the different options you have. Your purpose will make it easy to know when to say "yes" and when to say "no" as you move forward.

In addition to knowing your purpose, it's essential to have a vision for your future to keep you focused and to help you see what resources or new capabilities might be needed. Your vision is not an objective goal. It is subjective, meaning there is no one definition or recipe that tells you how to create it. Stay open and flexible by adapting to the possibilities that open up for you.

YOU CANNOT CHANGE WHAT YOU DO NOT ACKNOWLEDGE.

—DR. PHIL McGRAW

CHAPTER 6

ACCOUNTABILITY — OWNING YOUR RESULTS

All of us have had situations occur in our lives that have caused us to respond reactively or with resistance. The changes brought on by COVID are an example of being forced into circumstances we did not choose and had no control over. It is only natural to react and/or resist. In situations like these, it's easy to get distracted by the debate over how things should be. But focusing on that prevents us from taking an objective look at what is happening in our immediate circle of influence and asking ourselves the question, "How did I create this?"

When people hear the word "accountability," they sometimes think it means they did something wrong. Other people think of it as a way to keep score. Our world is filled with so much judgment and conflict. It seems like if we admit we are wrong, then we will be attacked or, at the very least, judged. Making it about blaming versus accounting is the first mistake we make.

This is why people resist looking at the results they have in their lives from an accountability perspective. The truth is that accountability creates awareness. And awareness opens the space for new learning that can lead to new actions and behaviors.

Accountability simply means to have ownership of all of our results. Most people love to take credit for the positive results they have created, telling us all the things they did to achieve them. However, they are reluctant to have that same sense of ownership when looking at the results they created that did not work for them. Simply put, accountability means that "I am able to account for the choices I made that led to the results I have."

Think of it like reviewing your bank account. You are able to see the choices that led to your account's current balance. You can see where perhaps you spent money on things that were not necessary and resulted in you having less money than you thought you had. If we never reviewed our bank statements, then we would never see how we could have made different choices.

When working with clients, I try to help them understand how being accountable can be empowering. Accountability provides an opportunity to access the power of creation — to be in the driver's seat of your life.

When you look at your results through a lens of accountability, you can determine what worked and what did not work. Being accountable also means you must be truthful

ACCOUNTABILITY SIMPLY MEANS TO HAVE OWNERSHIP OF ALL OF OUR RESULTS.

and avoid telling your "story" about a situation. By looking honestly at how the choices you made led to the results you have (both positive and negative), you can begin to see where you could have done some things differently. The old adage "hindsight is twenty-twenty" holds true.

Promises and Agreements

Over the years, I have coached many people on personal empowerment. At these training sessions, I begin with an activity that gets participants in alignment on agreements. I ask attendees to agree on how they will participate. First, I give each person a 5x7 index card and ask them to write on the front of the card their purpose for attending the training. Then, I ask them, "Why did you decide to be here?" Once they have written down their response on the card, I ask them to turn the card over and write down what attitudes and behaviors they are committed to demonstrating in order to achieve their desired outcome. I give them some ideas, like "I am committed to contributing." "I will have an open mind." "I commit to participating."

Once they have completed their card, I write two words on the easel — promise and agreement. And then I ask, "What is the difference between these two words?"

They think for a moment and then offer their thoughts, "A promise is something that is binding, like giving my word. Like when I got married." The group chuckles a bit.

"What about an agreement?" I ask.

Someone offers, "It's like when you make plans with your friends to get together at a certain time for lunch or dinner."

"Yes," I say, "But what is the difference between the two?"

"One is more important than the other," someone says. I can see some nodding of heads in the group.

Then I asked the group, "What is required to have an agreement or make a promise?"

They think for a moment, and I hear, "Some timeframe."

"Yes, what else?" I ask.

Someone replies, "A contract or something to sign that formalizes the promise, like when you sign your mortgage papers with the bank."

"Yes, all that is true. So, is there really any difference between the two?" I ask. I can begin to see the group reflecting.

I explain that both require one or more people to agree on something that will be completed, provided, or delivered to someone — under certain conditions and timeframes. When making a promise or agreement, we're taking accountability and acknowledging our responsibility for the specific actions we must take in order to fulfill our agreement.

HONORING OUR AGREEMENTS

In most instances, people perceive a promise as having more weight and being more important than an agreement. They see agreements as more casual or easily negotiated when, in fact, they are the same. Think of it this way. We often automatically say yes when people ask us to do something. I call this the bobblehead response, like the toy doll we used to buy and put in our cars. Very cute!

We say, "Yes, yes, yes," not stopping to consider what is required to fulfill the request (or agreement). Later, we may forget and then come up with an excuse for why we did not follow through. Most people accept this type of behavior when it comes to agreements. We may even make excuses for someone else, saying, "He told me he would be here. I guess something came up."

Let's get back to my personal empowerment training sessions. Once participants have an understanding of how agreements and promises are essentially the same, I ask them all to agree on how they will contribute during the training — be on time, share, raise their hand when they have a question, don't use cell phones, and no side talking. Everyone agrees that they will participate in this way to reduce distractions and create value for everyone.

At one particular training, we had taken a lunch break and agreed upon a specific time when everyone should return. A few minutes before the lunch break was ending, people started returning and taking their seats. I noticed four or five empty seats. I acknowledged all of those people who had kept their agreements and returned on time, and I began the lecture. Within five minutes, the remaining participants returned and were seated. I stopped to focus on those who returned late and asked them a simple question. "What could you have done to have gotten back from the lunch break on time?" Immediately, I saw people looking at each other with a questioning look, "Is she talking to me? I was on time." I could see that some people were feeling uncomfortable.

I stayed curious and neutral in my inquiry and waited for someone to respond. One man stood up and said, "I had to wait for my check at the restaurant."

Another person shared, "You can't expect him not to pay his bill."

"Of course not," I said, "Could he have gotten his check sooner?"

Someone who had come back late said, "I had to use the bathroom."

"Of course," I replied, "Could you have gotten back earlier to use the bathroom?"

This process is all about accountability. What I want people to see is that they had choices, and the choices they made led to the results they got. After spending time in the morning talking about promises and agreements, several still made choices that caused them to be late to the training and not keep their agreement to be on time.

THE IT FACTOR

Keeping our word to others can make or break trust. Our lives, careers, and relationships work exactly to the degree that we keep our agreements. Broken agreements create mistrust, disappointment, and broken relationships. Honoring our agreements and building trust creates self-confidence and also builds loyalty with others. The IT factor occurs when our integrity and trust are aligned. We do what we say we will do and build trustworthiness.

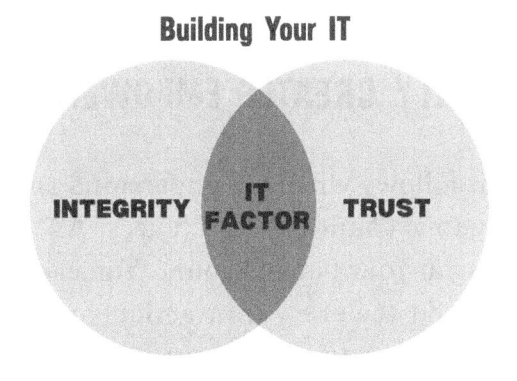

Building Your IT

INTEGRITY — IT FACTOR — TRUST

This is what I refer to as "rocks are hard, and water is wet." No one argues about this. These are facts — objective information. There is no judgment. It is what it is. However, when it comes to looking at the results we are creating, things can get subjective. We want to debate, give excuses, or tell our story to explain.

An agreement is a conscious pointing of intention toward a certain goal and then fulfilling that goal through commitment and actions. An agreement has integrity by virtue of the fact that we make it and keep it. Imagine your sphere of influence. What if no one took you seriously because they couldn't depend on you or believe in what you said? Your integrity and success rest on consistently keeping agreements — no excuses.

This is also the case when it comes to being true to our own purpose. The most profound agreements we make in life are those we make with ourselves. This may sound trite and simple, but it's the truth. If we can't keep promises to ourselves, how can we expect to keep them with others?

By staying committed, no matter what, to our word (our agreements and what we say we will do), we can trust ourselves more and create trust with others.

ACCOUNTABILITY CREATES EMPOWERMENT

Empowerment follows when we understand that each of us has the ability to account for our choices. As we discussed, it is like looking at your bank account. You can go back over the last month and see every transaction you made that led to the balance you have in your account. However, when it

THE MOST PROFOUND AGREEMENTS WE MAKE IN LIFE ARE THOSE WE MAKE WITH OURSELVES.

comes to looking at ourselves, our behaviors, and our attitudes, we are often resistant. The results are either good or bad, and we associate those results with our ego and image.

I often share the distinction between accountability and responsibility by using this example:

You are driving to work along the same route you take each day. You come to a red light and stop. As you are sitting in your car waiting for the light to change, a car comes up behind you and hits the rear end of your car. Are you accountable? Most people would say no. But I disagree and would tell them they are accountable. It's all about choices. They made all the choices that led to them sitting at that intersection at that time of day in their car. Are you responsible for the accident? No, of course not. The driver who hit you is responsible. You are accountable but not responsible.

Responsibility is having the ability to respond to any given situation. The driver who ran into the rear end of the car had the ability to respond in a different way, which could have prevented the accident from happening.

Could you have prevented being in the accident? Yes, by choosing to drive a different route or by leaving at a different time of day. Accountability is about choices, and responsibility is about how we respond to events. Understanding the difference between accountability and responsibility allows us to let go of the right/wrong assumptions and the blame game to learn how to make different choices and how to respond in different ways.

The Accountability Model I use with clients allows them to walk through a simple process in a neutral way. By answering a series of questions, they examine their choices more deeply, and they begin to see what they can do to change their results. Each time they walk through this model, there is new learning. They are empowered to declare a new choice and to take action, letting go of any negative feelings of disappointment or judgment about the results they created. Instead, they have new insights into understanding how their attitudes and behaviors get in the way of accomplishing what they want. They can begin to see how new attitudes, assumptions, and practices can be applied to get to where they want to go.

Own Your Results

As you create the change you want in your life, there will be times when you will not be successful. This is part of the process of change and makes it possible to create new practices or capabilities. It sets you up to change your life in ways that will support your future. None of us wake up in the morning and say, "How many mistakes can I make today?" But we do make mistakes.

When we make a mistake, this is the time to STOP and take accountability for the choices that got us here. What were some of the assumptions or attitudes that you had? "I assumed traffic would not be so bad." "I assumed that my project team member would provide the needed information to me on time so I could meet my deadline." "I was so excited and positive I didn't stop to think of what might happen."

We make choices based on our world view and how we see things. If things don't work the way you expect them to, don't play the blame game or make excuses. Look to see what you can learn so that in the future, you will make a different choice. Life is not perfect. We are not perfect. Be willing to acknowledge when you make a mistake — learn from it and move on.

Finally, behave with integrity and be conscious of the agreements you make. Taking responsibility for doing what you say you will do builds trust and a greater sense of self-confidence.

ACCOUNTABILITY MODEL

STOP	*Take a moment. Be neutral.*
LOOK	*Ask yourself — What were the attitudes, assumptions, and choices that led to this result?*
CHOOSE	*Do I want to keep making these choices, or do I want to make new ones? What else is possible?*
DECLARE	*Write down what you are up to NOW, and tell someone else.*
DO IT!	*Take committed action!*
STEP LEFT	*Move on — let go and see what shows up.*

PART 3

PUTTING IT ALL TOGETHER

IF YOU DON'T KNOW WHERE YOU ARE GOING, ANY PATH WILL TAKE YOU THERE.

—CHESHIRE CAT.
Alice in Wonderland

CHAPTER 7

CLEAR VISION AND COMMITMENT

Jim used to love to surprise me on my birthday each year by organizing a birthday trip. Since my birthday is on January 2 (yes, a Capricorn), no one wants to party after all of the holiday events. Pretty early on, Jim decided that a birthday trip would be a fun way to celebrate me and a good way to relax at the start of the year.

He would begin planning months in advance. We have traveled to Paris; London; Bend, Oregon, to ski; and even up the road to the Ritz Carlton, a mere thirty minutes away. On one trip, he blindfolded me before we got on the plane so that I couldn't see the boarding gate sign that showed where we were going. Once on board, Jim shared with the flight attendant, "This is a surprise birthday trip for my wife." Before the pilot announced where we were going, the flight attendant got on the mic and said, "We want to wish Barbara Fagan a happy birthday!" and then began leading the entire plane in singing, "Happy Birthday to you." Later, there was champagne for everyone in our section.

One of the things we would also do on these trips, besides having a great time relaxing and dining, was to talk about our lives. We would revisit the last year and share goals that we had achieved. We would discuss all that we had done both professionally and personally, from time spent with friends and family to the accomplishments in our busy work schedule.

I would often share with friends and associates that Jim and I were like bookends. I was born on January 2, two days after the start of the year, and he was born on the twenty-ninth, two days before the end of the month. Remember the 5th Dimension song "The Age of Aquarius"? Jim was the dreamer, and I was the goat, always butting his ideas into place. He was Mr. Positive, while I was more often Ms. Skeptic to his ideas. Together, we got things done, albeit with different approaches.

At the beginning of the year, it was always great to talk about our future. There is something about the quiet of the winter months that allows for stillness and time to reflect. Things seem to move at a slower pace after the frenzy of the holiday season. We would sit and talk over dinner about what we wanted in our future. We always imagined what our lives would look like in five years.

One year, we were sitting in a bistro in Paris and started to talk about our future. I think we were both having a sense of restlessness or perhaps a little boredom with our lives at that time. We had left our corporate roles, and I was actively coaching clients while Jim was working on his pet project remodeling houses. We really stretched ourselves to imagine what we wanted to create in the next five years.

The table in this bistro was covered with white butcher paper. As we talked, I began writing on the paper that covered the table all the things we were describing for our future — paying off all the credit cards, staying healthy, taking more trips to foreign locations, building my business, living in the California Wine Country someday, and even describing what our home would look like.

At the end of the evening, it was late, and things were starting to close down. As we left, I pulled the sheet of butcher paper from the table and brought it back home with me.

Three years later, in October 1991, we were involved in the Oakland Hills fire in which three thousand homes were lost. We had to evacuate that night and were only able to take a few things with us. The next morning, we were standing behind yellow tape that blocked the street, waiting to hear what had happened to our neighborhood. We found out that our house was still standing.

A few months later, Jim and I discussed our five-year plan and decided it was time for us to move to the Sonoma Wine Country. We spent a few months prepping the house and were fortunate to sell quickly to a family who had lost their home in the fire. They shared with us that our house reminded them so much of the house they had lost. It was a short escrow because they were anxious to move in and get settled after renting for several months.

While this was happening, Jim began driving to Sonoma County to find a realtor and look at some properties. We thought we had found a great fixer-upper, which would be an exciting project for Jim. Before we made an offer, we went up to meet with a contractor to estimate what a remodel would cost us.

While Jim and the contractor talked, I drove around to explore the beautiful roads of Healdsburg. I saw a for-sale sign on a property that we had not yet seen but was in the *Realtor* magazine. It was a bit more expensive than the house we were considering. Slowly, I drove up the long drive past two 1880s timber-framed barns. As I stopped at the base of a hill, I saw a beautiful white country colonial house on top of a knoll. I couldn't believe my eyes. It was so similar to our house in the Bay Area but with more of a country feeling about it.

This property was exactly how we had described the house we wanted in the Wine Country three years earlier at the bistro in Paris. I drove back to the fixer-upper and told Jim to get in the car so I could take him to see this property. When I drove up the drive past the barns, I could see the excitement on his face. He looked up at the house and said, "Whatever is wrong with that house, I can fix it." He did, and we lived there for almost thirty years, celebrating holidays with family and having large Fourth of July barbecues where everyone was welcome.

As I was cleaning out files in my office, preparing for our move to a smaller property, I came across a folded sheet of white paper. As I unfolded it, I recognized what it was. It was the butcher paper from the bistro table in Paris years ago. I sat down and read it, realizing we had created this over thirty years ago. I smiled, remembering that night and our excitement at what we had written down. Yes, we had achieved it all — living in the Sonoma Wine Country, paying off bills, having a wonderful extended family of friends and many adventures, trips to foreign countries, and good health all through the years.

5CS TO CREATING YOUR VISION

Together, Jim and I created a vision of what we wanted our future to look like. I do similar work with clients, helping them dream big and create a plan to achieve those dreams. One approach I like to use is what I call the 5Cs to achieve your vision. I have the 3P planning tools, so of course, I now have the 5Cs! What did you expect here?

Clarify Vision and Purpose

I believe that if you can imagine it, you can create it. When working with clients on their vision for their future, I encourage them to dream big, knowing that anything is possible. I have worked through this process myself and with clients many times, and I trust the process completely. What's challenging at the beginning is that people often only imagine the next year. Looking beyond that can seem unrealistic. However, that is where the real imagining takes over.

Consider this. Sometimes, people talk about a friend or colleague's success or achievement, and they assume the person was lucky or more fortunate. In my experience, people who achieve success work very hard and are guided and empowered by a clear vision and sense of purpose. Too often, people will make a decision and then, shortly afterward, doubt the decision they made. They start to question themselves. They listen to other people's opinions about what they are doing or planning and back away from what they really want.

SO WHAT NOW WHAT

5CS TO ACHIEVING YOUR VISION

Clarity	Purpose and Vision
Commitment	Set goals, take action, be accountable
Communicate	Enroll others, share your vision, limit negative self-talk
Collaborate	Align with others, and use all your resources
Celebrate	Acknowledge accomplishments along the way

Getting clear on your vision means taking the time to journal and reflect on what you want in life. It is the first step in designing your next chapter. Science has proven that as humans, we all have a brain, not just in our heads but also in our guts and in our hearts. This is why so many people do a gut check before making a decision. They also need to check within their heart to determine what is truly important to them.

It takes time to stop and be present with yourself. Quiet your mind, stop the busyness of your day, and give yourself time to spend in a reflective state. Listen closely to what your mind, heart, and gut are telling you. If you do this, you will know where you want to go and what you want to create in your next chapter. I have said to many clients, "If you don't think you are worthy or capable enough to have what you want, then you will never see the possibilities for you to achieve it."

No one has said that creating the life you want will be easy. However, it will be much easier and have a greater possibility of becoming a reality if you have clarity about what you really want. Giving yourself permission to dream and imagining your life filled with all that is important to you are gifts not many people give themselves.

As children, we dream about our future and what our lives will be like when we grow up. I can still remember as a little girl lying on the grass in the summer and looking up at the sky, feeling the warmth on my face as the sun shone down on me. I would see the big white clouds drifting by overhead, and as each cloud rolled over me, I would imagine it was a far-off land or maybe a big sailing boat or even, at times, a picture of a toy or bike or something that I really wanted.

Joseph Campbell, whom I have read and studied for years, has shared that Native Americans believed that what you played as a child is who you would become.[11] Imagination flourishes when we're very young, and many people stop imagining as they grow older. Keeping your imagination alive is something that we all can work on. In fact, our imagination often tells us what we really want, and it can be that simple. The key point is to listen and trust ourselves.

Commitment to Your Vision

Commitment is such a serious word. Do you ever notice yourself getting a little on edge when someone uses that word? Does it make you a little nervous? Does it give you a feeling of dread? We have all probably experienced some level of commitment, from marriage vows to work-related contracts to promises we've made. So, what does commitment really mean? How does it truly show up in our lives and relationships?

GIVING YOURSELF PERMISSION TO DREAM AND IMAGINING YOUR LIFE FILLED WITH ALL THAT IS IMPORTANT TO YOU ARE GIFTS NOT MANY PEOPLE GIVE THEMSELVES.

CLEAR VISION AND COMMITMENT

But before even beginning a discussion about commitment, the very first question to explore is, "What am I committed to?" Asking, "What am I committed to?" is different than saying, "What do I want?" A list of wants can be a pretty easy list to write out, but that's all it is: a list.

For instance, many websites allow users to create online wish lists where you can save a list of things you like (your wants). Obviously, they remain on the wish list until you or someone actually purchases the item, and it becomes a reality for you when it arrives on your doorstep. The want is the list, but the commitment is demonstrated when you actually make a purchase from that wish list, which results in you receiving what you want.

We only begin to see and experience real results when we move from wants and wishes to commitment (in the above example, a purchase). We may desire or want many things, but only with commitment do we create what we say we want.

Commitment requires getting clear about our intentions and making a promise to honor our word to ourselves and to others. But it's not always so easy. In addition to understanding our beliefs, attitudes, and assumptions, we also have to understand what may get in the way of acting on a commitment. What's happening when we're reluctant to commit or when we break our word?

While I believe that all humans are born whole and complete, we've learned ways to unconsciously create beliefs that cause us to doubt ourselves and our capabilities. Those beliefs create patterns that impact how we see and experience commitment. Identifying these patterns can help us begin to do things differently, especially around commitment.

Stay Persistent

Once you have allowed yourself to dream and clearly see your vision for the future, your commitment to that vision will be tested. I believe the universe throws obstacles in our way as a way to test our commitment. A Marvel movie is a great metaphor for what it takes to achieve your dream. Marvel heroes go through any and every obstacle thrown at them to demonstrate their commitment to what they want to achieve. To help your inner superhero, I recommend a few strategies to stay true to your commitment during challenging times.

Be Flexible. Being open to what shows up in your path is important. When I am set on creating something new in my life, I remind myself, "Not in my time, but in God's time." Being committed means staying flexible, being able to adapt, and being ready to course-correct. Most importantly, in the midst of that adaptiveness, you must never give up. Instead, remember that there can be many ways to get to where you want to go. Clarity and focus will get you most of the way, and determination will get you to the finish line.

Trust the Path. Surrender and trust that the path you take may not look like what you thought it would. By staying committed to the vision and paying attention to the opportunities that present themselves, you will see where and when to make choices that will move you toward your vision. I never thought it would take going through the Oakland Hills fire to end up in Sonoma Wine Country, where we had dreamed of living, but that is just the way it happened.

Take Action. Commitment shows up in action — not just thinking about what you want. The universe rewards our actions. People can say they are committed to something, but if that commitment isn't evident in their actions, then it is just a nice thought. Why is action important? Because without action, you have no results. We may not always create the results we want, but results are the only way we can measure our progress. Sometimes, it will feel like two steps forward and one step back, but at least you are moving.

Plan Toward Your Goal

People are sometimes afraid to set goals because they doubt they can achieve them, or they feel it will be too hard, or they just don't know what to do. I can tell you with one hundred percent certainty that the only way to move toward what you want is to create a plan and set goals. That is the only way you will be able to measure how you are moving toward your vision. Write down the milestones or interim goals that you need to accomplish to attain your goal. These steps will move you in the right direction. Then, ask yourself every month, "How am I doing on my goals?"

Asking this question pushes you to look at the results you are creating, evaluate their effectiveness, and then take action. If your results aren't in alignment with what you want, then stop and reconsider — what is another way to get where you want to go? When committed to something truly important to us, we can get very creative and try things that we have never done before. Take the leap and try something new to get where you want to go.

If you are not committed, it can be easy to find an excuse. I call this the "Yeah, but" redirect — I would have had it, but ... I could have done it, but ... I wanted to do it, but ... Whenever I hear one of my clients saying "but," I know a story or an excuse is likely to follow.

The "Yeah, but" habit is an easy one to fall into. I often encourage my clients to create a no "but" zone, meaning that word is off-limits. I suggest they get a glass jar and keep it near them. Then, they let their family and friends know that they are creating a no "but" zone. Every time they or someone else catches them saying "but" in any sentence, they need to put twenty-five cents (or more!) in the jar. They pretty quickly become more conscious of how they make excuses for not taking action or completing something.

Communicate Your Vision

There is something powerful and sometimes scary about sharing out loud what we want. This is probably because communicating our vision for our future out loud means we then have witnesses who will hear us and remind us of what we have declared. But once shared, it reminds us that this is the kind of declaration that evokes commitment. It is real and important and not just something you should do or what someone else thinks you should do. Declarations like these come from a place deep inside you that speaks to fulfilling your purpose in life and supports your values and the quality of life you intend to have.

Years ago, I was attending a reunion conference with all the coaches I've trained over the years. It was great fun hearing them share all that they were doing and seeing the growth they had achieved as professional coaches.

At the end of the conference, we shared our declarations of what we were going to create in the future. There were declarations about how many clients someone would have, speaking engagements they would create, or how they would grow their coaching practice. I shared that I would be writing a book. This was something that I had been encouraged to do for many years, but by making that declaration, I had created witnesses. They all knew that I coached people to take action on their declarations based on their commitment, so I was not going to get off the hook on this one.

Collaborate With Others

A year after that conference, I got an e-mail from Bernadette, one of Source Point Training's Leadership Coaches. She said, "Hi Barbara, how is your book coming?"

My first reaction was, "Sh#*, I haven't taken any action." I responded by saying, "I have been busy, and I am spending a lot of time planning what I will be writing."

She quickly responded, "Great! I'm really looking forward to reading it."

This inquiry happened every year for several years. Bernadette is a great coach, and I am happy to have her commitment to my declaration. Not often do we have someone who will remind us and keep encouraging us to create what we say we want in our lives.

Of course, I had many excuses or stories about why I had not written a book yet, but those didn't matter. What mattered is that I had made a declaration, and I had not taken action. I spent a lot of time evaluating what I wanted to write and, in fact, took time to write a book outline, but

I stopped myself due to a multitude of circumstances I'd been dealing with. The main fact was that I had not yet committed to writing.

When we share what we want to create in our lives, we attract more resources to support us. If I tell my friends, "I want to buy a new car," then suddenly people are sharing with me different types of cars I might like or special deals they've seen. Someone might hear about a great car for sale or even just ask me for more details about what kind of car I want to buy. This kind of collaboration propels us forward, and we have more people supporting us to achieve our goals.

Celebrate Achievements

Take time to celebrate all the achievements you make as you design your next chapter. Recognizing your progress is empowering. No matter how small or large the accomplishment, recognize it. When we positively acknowledge ourselves, we gain confidence.

Creating change can be scary, and we all have moments of self-doubt. We may expect the worst and can get into feelings of fear and scarcity. At times like these, I have a few strategies.

My favorite approach is to turn on some great tunes and dance around the house to move my body and clear my energy. I always say, "Move your body, and your mind will follow." It makes me feel more positive, and then I'm reenergized and ready to continue exploring the new territory I am in.

When self-doubts arise, affirmation cards are also useful. They can help you reflect and refocus. I often buy them for my clients to help them stay positive about the changes they are making. Hay House is one company that creates cards that are all about celebrating who you are — mind, body, and spirit.

Sometimes, seeing is believing, and creating a vision map can be a fun, visual way to celebrate the future you intend to create (like my butcher paper from that bistro long ago). Vision maps often combine written and visual elements to remind you of what you want in your life. Some of my clients have created beautiful collages and even framed them.

When you reach a milestone on your path to your future, acknowledge yourself and find ways to celebrate. There are many little things that you can do to recognize your effort, which can empower you to keep going and believe in the future you want to create.

Integrated Change Model

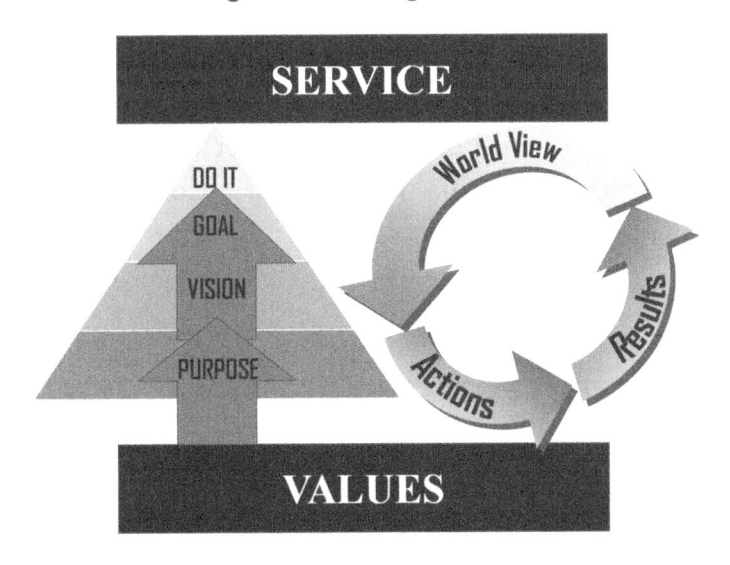

Putting It Together

When we have identified our purpose for our next chapter and have a clear vision of what we intend to create, we can then begin to set the goals that will move us forward. Our actions are the smallest part of this process. Once we have clarity of vision and have set goals, then we can take action and DWIT — Do Whatever It Takes!

Of course, there will be tests along the way, but by staying true to our purpose and guided by our vision and values, we will adapt and keep going. When challenges seem overwhelming, we need to remember to use all our resources and ask for support from friends, family, and perhaps a coach.

At this point, there is no going back to where we were. We have challenged our world view and are able to see things from a new perspective and identify new possibilities. Perhaps we will need to develop new skills and capabilities as we change. You are beginning to plant the seeds for your future. You will start to realize you are the gatekeeper and caretaker of your next chapter. But we will also have a new sense of self-confidence and begin to become comfortable as this new chapter unfolds.

STEPS TO DESIGNING YOUR FUTURE

- Make space and time to dream. Take a trip or even sit in a museum and be inspired by masters. Take a tablet and make notes. Do not write down things to do. Instead, write about what your dream will look and feel like once you have achieved it. What is that "one-day" conversation you keep repeating to yourself? What is the spirit you want to bring to your life each day — optimistic, pragmatic, curious, adventurous?
- Imagine yourself in the future. See all aspects of your life. Think about your career, your friends and relationships, health, service and contribution activities, educational opportunities, challenging projects you would like to take on, and the new capabilities you will develop. If your life were to unfold just the way you want it to, where would you be living? What would you be doing? Who would be in your life?
- What are your unique gifts, and how do you want to contribute with those gifts? If you had all the time you wanted, how would you spend your time?
- Allow yourself to dream BIG. If you feel a little fear or have a big gulp in your throat while imagining achieving your dream, GOOD!
- Anytime we think of achieving something big for ourselves, we must realize that all things will change around us as well.
- Consider your core values. Think of your vision as being in alignment with your life and the legacy you will create. Achieving your vision will give you not

just a sense of achievement but also something that will impact others and the world around you.
- Put it all together. Write one concise statement in your notebook that describes what your vision will look like once it's realized. The big one for us was:
    "Someday, we will live in a beautiful country setting in the California Wine Country, where our extended family will love to visit and where we can contribute to an active community of friends and business associates."
- Declare it out loud to others. Let people know what your vision is and what action you are taking to move toward it.
- Create a big, bold, bodacious (BBB) goal for the year ahead. This goal must be tied to your vision. How will this goal move you toward achieving your vision?

I WANT YOU TO GET EXCITED ABOUT WHO YOU ARE, WHAT YOU ARE, WHAT YOU HAVE, AND WHAT CAN STILL BE FOR YOU. I WANT TO INSPIRE YOU TO SEE THAT YOU CAN GO FAR BEYOND WHERE YOU ARE RIGHT NOW.

—VIRGINIA SATIR

CHAPTER 8

COMMUNICATE TO WIN

Years ago, I was traveling to different cities in the United States, working with parents of at-risk teens. In groups, we would discuss a lot of sensitive, emotional topics, like home life and family dynamics. I was surprised that I could almost immediately tell if parents were sharing or communicating from a place of personal responsibility or not. I sensed whether they were open to learning new ways of parenting or if they were defensive about their situation.

This intuition led me to research how people communicate not just in the family dynamic but also in businesses and organizations. I understood that what we say and how we say it reflects how we interpret life, but I wanted to understand the disconnect between our words and our meanings. What was making it so hard for people to understand each other?

When reading Virginia Satir, a researcher renowned for her work on how people and families communicate with each other, it became more clear. She addresses how our words express our inner feelings and beliefs, but many of us are unaware of how what we say is received and understood. Instead, we react to the responses we get from others but rarely ask listeners if the intent of our communication was understood. [12] I often hear people say to others, "That is not what I meant." Or "You don't understand what I am saying." When our intent is not understood, it's important to figure out what happened.

This is especially true in the business world. Many teams talk about productivity, but they don't speak productively. I've been in many meetings where time is spent discussing issues without reaching an agreement. The meeting ends with no clarity on who will do what and when it needs to be completed. When this occurs, assumptions can be made, which can lead to missed deadlines, lack of further communication, and an increase in unresolved issues.

People are guided by corporate culture and quickly learn what to say and what not to say. In Peter Lencioni's book, *The Five Dysfunctions of a Team*, he talks about the importance of trust and safety in a team. He describes high-performing teams as having the ability to have honest and healthy debates in order to generate the best decisions and outcomes. Without trust, communication is guarded.[13]

In this chapter, I cover common roadblocks to effective communication and provide solutions and techniques that can help you manage and improve communication.

MANY TEAMS TALK ABOUT PRODUCTIVITY, BUT THEY DON'T SPEAK PRODUCTIVELY.

POWERFUL REQUESTS

People spend a good amount of time complaining about things — life, jobs, relationships, health, finances. I've discovered that these complaints are, more often than not, a way someone expresses a desire for change. When a client starts to complain about their circumstances, I immediately ask, "What do you want? When do you want it?" And "Who do you want it from?" Asking these types of specific questions helps channel discontent into a solvable framework.

It helps them ask the type of questions that can change the game. Powerful requests are pretty straightforward but require a few specific elements:

1. Committed speaker
2. Committed listener
3. Conditions to be fulfilled (The Ask)
4. Specific timeframe
5. Response - yes, no, or counteroffer

While these elements of an effective request seem quite simple, I am fascinated by how few people actually know how to make a complete request.

For example, I've often sat in on client meetings where the manager says, "We need to get these reports done." The faces around the table all have a blank stare as if to say, "What reports? Who needs to get them done? When do they need to get them done?" Amazingly, however, all heads nod in agreement, but no clear agreement has actually been made.

Learning to speak specifically and objectively helps people understand what you want. For instance, if you say to someone, "I would like you to help me with this project." That is unclear and subjective. The other person doesn't know specifically what you want them to do. In contrast, if you say, "I would like you to spend one hour with me this afternoon reviewing the timeframe for implementing project X and providing your input." That is specific and objective. Your listener knows exactly what you want, how much time you need, and what they will provide. The greater the clarity, the easier it is to create agreements and understanding of expectations.

THE ART OF ENROLLMENT

In order to be successful, enrollment is an art that most great salespeople have mastered. Simply put, it's the process of encouraging others to work with you by aligning them with your goals. When creating change in your life and making big decisions, enrollment is critical. None of us can ever achieve success alone, and enrollment helps us access resources that can support us.

Small children learn enrollment at a young age, usually because they are so cute and hard to deny, but also because they have not faced much rejection. As we get older, we often fear enrolling others in our vision and asking for support because we don't want to experience rejection. Of course, this has to do with our self-worth. "Am I worthy of the support that I need?" is a thought we have that can stop us from asking for what we want.

But life is all about enrollment. Either someone is enrolling you, or you are enrolling them. Enrolling others to support your vision or help create the change you want to make is really about creating alignment. It's about communicating your intent to the listener, and it's the most essential part of any successful enrollment process.

With my clients, I often share the RAISE enrollment model as a technique to help empower them and create effective alignment with others.

RAISE Enrollment Model

Relate – Begin by creating rapport with the person you are enrolling. Find something that you both can relate to or have in common. This might be referred to as small talk.

Align – Start by asking them if they have time to talk with you. Explain what you want to talk about (intent), and see if they have time to discuss it (or plan another time to meet). Don't start by telling them what you want. People want to feel they have a choice and appreciate that you respect their time.

Inquire – Check in during the discussion to see if they are interested in what you are asking from them. How would they like to support you? Do they have any questions that would help them decide to work with you?

Support – Relationships are all about mutual support. Let them know how their contribution or support will benefit both of you. Tell them how you intend to support them as well.

Engage – Here's where the rubber meets the road. Ask them, "Will you do this? When can we begin?" If you never ask specific questions about next steps and how they will take action, you'll never know if they are enrolled.

I have seen many people skip the first step when relating to others (building rapport) and go right to telling people what they want or need. This does not work because there is no alignment or sense of partnership and support. In our fast-paced world, we sometimes forget the art of dialogue, which can show up in our text messages, zoom meetings, and awkward face-to-face conversations.

DIFFICULT CONVERSATIONS

Many of us have been kept awake late at night, replaying conversations in our heads. The dialogue may relate to a conflict with someone at work or perhaps a disagreement with a partner or friend. When we don't know how to address these unresolved conflicts, we tend to hold onto them. It can feel like a ticking time bomb that we are afraid will go off if we initiate the conversation. Instead, we replay it in our head over and over until it gets to the point of potential hostility and explosion. The odds of starting a neutral conversation at this point are slim to none.

No one likes conflict, and some people are more conflict-averse than others. And, as hard as it may seem, part of responsible communication involves learning how to have difficult conversations. You may never like to have these conversations; however, there are some useful techniques that can make them go more smoothly and cause you less stress.

Ask for What You Want

The definition of a difficult conversation varies for each of us — asking someone to repay you, asking for a raise, returning an item to a store, telling your spouse you want more intimacy (a.k.a. sex), or telling someone you are not interested in them. The level of discomfort the situation gives us usually predicts how long we wait to have this conversation.

However, the more difficult the conversation is, the more important it is to have. The best approach involves three elements:

- Plan a specific time to have the conversation.
- Be clear about what you need to say.
- Prepare so you are able to discuss the issue neutrally.

I often work with clients to prepare them for these difficult conversations and suggest the following tips to help successfully navigate them.

Get grounded and shift to neutral. What is your story about the situation? Take time to make notes or journal about your perspective. Identify how you feel.

Consider the other person's point of view. What is their story about the situation? What do they want? Work to challenge yourself to get out of your position and see their perspective.

What would be a third person's perspective? If a third person heard both stories, what might their perspective of the situation be?

Approach the other person with the belief that they are open to talk. Let them know you want to have a clearing conversation about the issue. No one likes to feel attacked, so don't start the conversation with your guns blazing.

Speak objectively versus subjectively. State the facts as you see them. Don't speak subjectively by beating around the bush. People look for clarity when being confronted about a conflict. Cite a real example of what happened rather than talking about how you feel about it. As the detective used to say on an old TV show, "Give me the facts, just the facts." Ask the other person how they see the situation or if there is anything you have shared that is different than their perspective.

Make a specific request. What do you want? Be clear with the other person about what you want them to do or not do going forward.

Continue to discuss until you have reached an agreement. Keep an open mind and consider both perspectives about the situation being discussed. As Stephen Covey advises in his book *Seven Habits of Highly Successful People*, "Seek first to understand before being understood." Listen and keep an open mind.[14]

Plan to follow up. Schedule to meet in person, if possible, to see if the situation that created the conflict has gotten better. This is always a good idea as it helps to maintain the relationship and rebuild trust.

ORGANIZATIONAL CHANGE

So far, I've discussed ways to improve interpersonal communication skills, and now, I'd like to spend time discussing my philosophy on how these skills can be used to manage organizational change. I have spent the better part of my coaching career working with organizations managing change, which can get messy. As I've coached clients through this process, I've discovered it requires careful listening and setting a clear purpose.

Platinum Software is a great example of a company that has navigated organizational change. I started working with them shortly after they went public. The good news is that the company was growing faster than expected following an infusion of capital from investors. They went from eighty employees to eight hundred and fifty in ten months.

The bad news is that the company was being run by the original founding partners — three young and very ambitious men who had brilliant ideas but not a great deal of business background. The CEO was a pied piper of sorts, extremely masterful at enrolling new business partners. During this time, he bought and acquired five companies.

The original product was designed and developed by a tight-knit group of employees who delivered the product at a price point of $290 through resellers with great dealer relationships. Now, they had become a public corporation and were selling $250K products directly to businesses. This is when the "Armani Suits" arrived, which is what the new sales team had been dubbed. They were hired from firms like McKinsey and Anderson Consulting.

Around this time, I met Dana while she was working at Platinum. She was known as the fix-it person. She worked long hours like everyone else, putting out fires and trying to keep teams from killing each other. Because new companies were being acquired and new employees continually added, there were no shared values or vision. Merging teams with different corporate cultures and simultaneously trying to integrate what they were doing created a great deal of confusion. Dana tried to communicate with the leadership team, saying, "We can't keep doing this. These young people can't keep up and don't have the experience to deal with this type of growth."

However, the company continued changing without a clear strategy for growth or the systems and processes in place needed to support it. As each department grew, more and more conflicts arose about how each team would work together to facilitate the delivery of products and services.

I was called in to meet with the founders, who described to me the growing pains the company was having. One by one, I met with each department head to assess their perspective about what was not working. The overall complaint was that communication between departments was poor. It felt like a group of different families living under the same roof (corporation) who did not want to support each other and who just wanted to be left alone to do things their own way.

When I first met Dana, she was head of the Quality Assurance department. Quality Assurance had the ultimate authority to determine when a product was ready to be released and go to market. This was a problem for the sales team, who could not seem to get products to their customers fast enough. The sales team was always breathing down the neck of the quality assurance team to approve a product so they could get it out there and make money.

One day, I went to meet with Dana, and she jumped up from her desk and said, "I get it!"

"What?" I asked.

She went to her music system, which she always had on in her office, and searched for the song she wanted me to hear. Soon, I began to hear Barbra Streisand singing "Children Will Listen." As I listened to the words, I asked Dana, "What did you get from this song?"

She said, "It's like being a parent. Children always watch what their parents are doing. They hear what their parents are saying, even when they don't know they are listening. It's not about what we are doing. It's about how we are being with each other."

"Yes," I said, " that is what we have been discussing these last few weeks."

As I worked with Dana and her team, she began to give feedback to each team member about how they were communicating with their counterparts on other teams. She pointed out ways they could start to communicate more effectively with each other to build trust and cooperation. I could begin to see a change occur.

Teams started listening to each other. They spent time at the beginning of each meeting to establish a clear purpose for the meeting and then identified specific outcomes they wanted from the meeting. Alliances were formed on how the different teams could work together to increase trust and commitment and to work towards a shared goal.

When attending a meeting with other teams, they practiced objective and accountable communication by setting deadlines and making commitments for when they would complete their part of a project. The best part? They met the deadlines and commitments. Trust began to grow across the interdependent teams.

After a few days in the office working with teams, I would occasionally meet with the founders. One day, one of them said to me, "You know, Barbara, I can tell which teams you have been working with by the way they communicate." I considered that a compliment.

Dana went on to start her own company and applied all that she had learned from this experience. Teams worked together, listened to each other, and focused on their shared purpose and goals. They celebrated achievements together, and as they grew, they were able to sustain shared values with a clear mission. They understood what it meant to be accountable to one another.

Having worked with many CEOs and senior executives over the years, I have a great deal of compassion for the work required to navigate businesses, large and small, through times of change. An expanding business presents one challenge, but downsizing is another difficult challenge. During the Great Recession of 2007–2009, everyone was impacted — homeowners, banks, and many businesses.

At one late meeting, I was sitting with department heads charged with determining who would be laid off in the upcoming weeks. There was a lot of emotion, anger, and frustration. No one wanted to make the hard decisions. Most were trying to protect their employees from being on the list, but decisions needed to be made. At the end of the meeting, after some tough decisions were made, someone asked, "Now what are we going to do with a smaller workforce? How will we keep our customers and revenue on track?" That would be another long, late-night meeting.

At times like these, when organizations face changes that will impact all employees, people begin to come together to support each other. Through creative conversations, new ideas can be floated and tried, with many being successful.

Trust is the key ingredient in organizational change. The walls come down, and there is an experience of authenticity, knowing they are all in it together. I encourage teams to talk about trust all the time to become clear on their values and how they will work together.

UNLESS THE TEAM WINS, NO ONE WINS

Business team coaching is one of the fastest-growing areas for business coaching professionals. In order to create high-performance teams or teams that are truly self-sustaining, a strong base of trust must be developed among team members. They need to know that there are no solo players. Unless the team wins, no one wins.

This requires managers to make a significant mindset shift. Over the last ten years, more and more organizations have invested in professional coach training, where in-house coaches are available to support both individuals and teams at all levels.

In one of our most recently developed trainings, Business Team Coach, I share the fundamental principle of team coaching. Teams must consider themselves one entity with many moving parts. They must understand that what one part of the team is doing impacts the entire team. By working together in this way, they feel much more responsible for the decisions and actions they are taking in supporting their role on the team.

Managers are typically used to running team meetings. In team coaching, the more the manager is able to turn the meeting over to the team, the greater the team's ownership and peer support. The team will develop in order to become successful. For many managers, this feels like letting go of control, which it is at some level. However, it is really about empowering the team and trusting the team to make decisions, though this is not to say a manager should allow a team free-for-all. Empowering the team involves some structure:

- All teams need to be set up to understand what game they are playing. What is the team's purpose?
- What are the team rules that they agree to play by? This requires aligning the team on values and discussing how their values will be demonstrated in the team's attitudes and behaviors.
- The team needs to know how they will keep score. They need to know, at all times, where they are on a project, what the deadlines are, what needs to change in order to meet the team goals, and who is responsible for each part of the team's deliverables.

Accountability and ownership of personal and shared responsibilities are the hallmarks of today's high-performing teams. Understanding, knowing, and implementing these pieces of team management will result in success. Teams that don't know how to keep score will ultimately lose.

The degree of responsibility we take for our communication directly relates to how our relationships will work. It is too easy to blame others for not understanding us or hearing what we say. I often say the following when coaching clients,

"The meaning of your communication is the response that you get." If you are not getting the response you want from your communication, then stop and consider another way to communicate in order to be heard.

Communication is what connects us as humans, and surprisingly, communication often is not based on the words that we use — it has to do with our tone, our physical presence, our assumptions, and our judgments. Stay curious, stay open, and really spend time listening to people. You will be amazed at what you can learn.

SOMETHING VERY BEAUTIFUL HAPPENS TO PEOPLE WHEN THEIR WORLD HAS FALLEN APART; A HUMILITY, A NOBILITY, A HIGHER INTELLIGENCE EMERGES AT JUST THE POINT OUR KNEES HIT THE FLOOR.

—MARIANNE WILLIAMSON

CHAPTER 9

BREAKDOWN TO BREAKTHROUGH

Each of us has faced breakdowns in our lives, some more significant than others. When they occur, we can become overwhelmed and confused. There's a sense of impossibility to the situation that makes one feel lost, uncertain about what to do, and very much alone.

The night I lost Jim, I could barely function. Everything I had thought about how I would handle his passing completely disappeared. For days, I became someone I did not even recognize. I had never faced such pain. In my head, I tried to tell myself, "This is God's will, and I have done everything I can to make sure he had a gentle passing." But that didn't help. All I knew was that my life was now forever changed. I had no clue, at that moment, about how to move forward. We dread breakdowns like these because they throw us into a place of uncertainty, self-doubt, and fear.

We generally exist with a false sense of security or control over our surroundings. When faced with breakdowns, the fear button gets pushed. For me, I ceaselessly asked questions throughout Jim's treatments. My "I need to know" response was all I thought about as Jim's disease progressed. I read every medical report, scan, lab test, and doctor's report in an effort to know exactly what was happening. I kept thinking, "If I just know more, I'll be able to manage the situation so it won't get too bad."

I knew this thinking was just a reaction to the circumstances of what was happening. No matter how much I knew, the likelihood of things turning out as I wanted them to was slim. There were so many changes — late-night visits to the hospital and the anxiety of wondering and waiting for results to return so I could know what to expect. There were times I honestly believed, "I have a handle on this. I am managing pretty well."

During that time, no one stopped to tell me how tired or even desperate I looked. Everyone saw it, but I was so focused on trying to maintain control I couldn't see it. Breakdowns can create moments of desperation, trying to manage through the storm and waiting for things to quiet down so that we can feel we are in control again.

THE ONLY WAY OUT IS THROUGH

The only way to get out of a breakdown is to go through it.

When my mom left my dad, I was twenty-five years old. All three of us (the kids) were out of the house and had lives of our own, and my Mom decided she could no longer deal with my dad's drinking. It was affecting his health and his ability to function at work.

With the help of Al-Anon, she had started to understand that her life and health were more important than enabling an alcoholic. She committed to taking a stand for herself and left the home she had lived in for twenty years. My sisters and I were a bit miffed, thinking, "Why didn't she do that earlier while we were at home?" We had lived through many drunken fights and late-night arguments.

My sisters and I helped her move into an apartment across town. We visited with our dad and encouraged him to get help, telling him how much we loved him and Mom. A year passed, and eventually, he did get help. He became an active participant in a local Alcoholics Anonymous (AA) group and even went on to sponsor many alcoholics. Another year passed, and my mom moved back home with my dad. They both stayed active members of their AA community for many years. Alcoholism is pervasive, and I have been guarded most of my adult life, fearing that the demon of addiction would reside within me.

My years of coaching experience have taught me that the ability to acknowledge and face breakdowns is a good thing. We generally don't like breakdowns, and in fact, we're likely to do everything we can to avoid them. But breakdowns are inevitable, and in fact, a breakdown often reflects our commitment. When we're powerfully committed to something, we will face challenges or breakdowns. The funny thing is that if we aren't committed, then nothing really matters, and we don't experience a breakdown.

Declaring what you are committed to establishes what you might do in certain situations and requires you to take actions that honor your declaration. We make declarations about what we are committed to changing in our lives, and then the universe challenges our commitment to what we have declared. "I am going to lose weight! Oh no, now I can't enjoy my daughter's wedding events — the bachelorette party, bridal shower, rehearsal dinner, and the Big Day. There will be so much great food to enjoy. How can I not eat?"

Yes, commitment means we will be challenged. In order to work our way around any challenging situation, we must be committed. Plato said, "Necessity is the mother of invention."[15] I say, "Breakdown is the mother of invention" because breakdown creates the opportunity for a breakthrough.

EMBRACING BREAKDOWNS

The first step when dealing with a breakdown is to declare it. Ignoring it will not change anything. In fact, things tend to get worse if you do. The second step is to declare your commitment to clearing up the breakdown. This typically requires working with the people involved to identify the source of the breakdown and then beginning to take the necessary steps to resolve it.

I once worked with a woman who had just been promoted to a new management position. She was responsible for managing an initiative that involved many local community agencies. She shared with me that there was one person who reported to her and whom she interacted with on a weekly basis. He was responsible for providing specific data for the project but would often be late to weekly meetings and, at times, did not provide the

BREAKDOWN IS THE MOTHER OF INVENTION.

required data. In fact, she felt he was not committed to the project because he did not seem interested when he came to the meetings, looking at his cell phone messages while she was talking.

I spent time sharing with her what I call the Breakdown Clearing Process. It's a model I have frequently and successfully used with clients that is meant to resolve breakdowns in communication.

BREAKDOWN CLEARING PROCESS

1. Declare the breakdown to those involved.
2. Declare your commitment to clear up the breakdown.
3. Invite others to participate with you to resolve the breakdown.
4. Listen to all points of view with an open mind.
5. Identify the source of the breakdown:
   - Lack of training
   - Lack of confidence, trust
   - Lack of appropriate systems or practices
   - Lack of resources — time, materials, finances
   - Lack of commitment
   - Lack of planning or strategies
6. Brainstorm solutions.
7. Agree on a plan.
8. Set up a time to follow up.

At first, she was hesitant to take on having this type of conversation with the employee. She felt that if she raised the issue, things could get worse. I encouraged her to think more positively. If she approached him with her commitment to resolve the breakdown, spoke with an open mind, and invited his partnership, she might be surprised by his response.

When we met the following week, she shared, "I was so nervous, but I did talk to him. You were right. I was surprised, but we had a great conversation." She told me that he had said he knew he hadn't been participating fully in the initiative. This caused him a lot of stress because he knew how important the project was. He was afraid to admit this because his wife was very ill. He had so many things going on at home with his two teenage daughters that he was trying to find help. When my client heard this, she immediately felt compassion for him. They were able to brainstorm ways for him to find help at home and also how to get assistance at work in order to collect the needed data for the project.

Breakdown to Breakthrough

Commitment → BREAK DOWN → Breakthrough

Ego
Fear
Self-Doubt

Lack of Experience
Lack of Commitment
Lack of Resources

BARRIERS TO PERFORMANCE

When things aren't going the way we want, we may stop ourselves, shut down, and give up. This is especially true when we are taking new ground, like looking for a new job, moving, finding a home to buy, seeking a new relationship, or saving money. In these challenging moments, we can become paralyzed and stop ourselves from moving forward.

Perhaps our ego has gotten bruised in our attempt to "Go for it!" When this happens, each of us demonstrates certain attitudes — a favorite response and behavior we default to when things aren't working out. These habits are extensions of our temperament and personality. In coaching, I refer to these attitudes as "barriers to performance."

BARRIERS TO PERFORMANCE

Self-doubt – "What was I thinking?"
Skeptic – "This will never work."
Victim – "Everybody else wins but me."
Confusion – "I just don't know where to begin."
Righteous – "This isn't what I really wanted anyway."

Attitudes

I am a firm believer that our attitude creates our experience. If I embody a losing attitude, then the interactions I have with people, even my physical way of being, can present me as a loser, which then becomes a self-fulfilling prophecy.

OUR ATTITUDE CREATES OUR EXPERIENCE.

Remember the enrollment section? We're constantly enrolling others. We can enroll others in our negative conversations, our reasons, stories, and excuses about why we haven't achieved what we want. Giving up is easy, and we have become used to hearing people's victim stories. In fact, it can actually be easier to accept people's failures rather than celebrate their successes. It is no wonder that the way we respond to our circumstances is rarely challenged.

As I listen to clients talk about their experiences, I find their responses fall into one of five categories: self-doubt, skeptic, victim, confusion, or righteousness. When describing to me the results they have created, their voice reveals their attitude.

To someone experiencing **self-doubt**, I say, "What is one step you can take today that you can feel confident about?" There is usually at least one thing they can think of, and I encourage them to do that one thing. I remind people that action creates energy — no action, more self-doubt.

To the **skeptic**, I say, "What haven't you tried yet?" They might respond by saying, "I've tried everything." "Everything?" I will ask. "Can you think of one thing that you haven't tried?" This gets them to pause and think, "What haven't I tried?" Again, they can usually think of one thing, and I encourage them to give it a try.

The most common barrier to performance for many of us is a feeling of failure. Like a **victim**, people feel like "no one wants to help me, and every time I try something new, this happens." The feeling of failure is a real performance killer. I often reframe this by saying, "What happened is not failure. It is feedback. What could you have done differently?" Examining results we didn't want opens up the possibility of learning. When we are not successful, we can use the feedback and try something different.

My response, at times, is generally not sympathetic to those who are really stuck and want to be right about failing. To redirect this attitude, I may ask, "If you weren't focusing on what you can't do, what could you do?" This usually interrupts the victim energy, and I can get a little fight out of people in their response.

Confusion is a barrier to performance because it literally stops us. Our brains say, "I am confused. I don't know what to do, so therefore, I can't do anything." I have a simple response to this, "What are you confused about?" "I don't know" is the answer. To that, I say, "I don't know, is not an answer. What are you confused about?" It's time to delve deeper and figure out what is causing the confusion.

Righteous responses are deflections that prevent dialogue. This is my preferred barrier to performance and may result in comments like, "What do you expect me to do? Do you think I am an idiot?" Notice the self-limiting belief playing through my righteous response. Yup, it is always there. To that, I would say, "What are you trying to be right about?"

Breakdowns will always challenge our commitment. Giving up is easy, but continuing to find ways to achieve goals is where real breakthroughs occur. This type of resilience is how many organizations achieve success as they grow, evolve, and change. They take time to look and see what is happening and then evaluate the results being created. They are willing to declare the breakdown. Then, they are willing to be responsible for enrolling others to identify the source of the breakdown and create change with new actions, policies, or processes. They also examine the attitudes, barriers, and behaviors of those involved and identify what needs to shift in order to create a new level of performance and results.

LIFE IS LIKE AN ELEVATOR. WHEN YOU GO UP A LEVEL, THERE WILL ALWAYS BE SOMEONE OR SOMETHING NEW TO GREET YOU.

CHAPTER 10

PRINCIPLES OF ACCOMPLISHMENT

I have found there are key principles that guide successful people to accomplish what they want in life. These principles set us up to make better choices and help us let go of our ego and right/wrong thinking. They can lead you to success, but this requires introspection, action, and work.

Many times, people don't think about how they became successful, which is unfortunate. They don't spend time reflecting on the attitudes and behaviors that led them to achieve what they wanted in life. When working with clients, I explain how commitment, willingness, and discipline lead to great results. I've used these principles of accomplishment to help them see the opportunities they have to accomplish their goals.

COMMITMENT

Commitment requires action. There are ways that we can tell when people are committed. They declare what they intend to create, and they enroll others in their projects and vision. They get clear about the steps required and stay focused while being willing to be flexible and adapt as they move towards their goals. They do whatever it takes and commit to creating what they want.

Make a Plan

Whatever you envision for your next chapter, you must commit to it, and you'll need a plan to get it done. Know your purpose, create your vision, and set goals. Use this foundation to create a game plan to move you toward what you want. If you don't begin with a solid vision and purpose, your goals will just feel hard and become "have-to-dos" rather than "want-to-dos." When guided by this structure and motivated by a strong purpose, we are more likely to hold ourselves accountable and continue to find ways to move forward, no matter what challenges show up.

Setting goals is another way to ensure we continue to find ways to move forward. Goals are objective. We achieve them, or we don't. They serve as guideposts along the way. In fact, our goals are like stepping stones to our vision. Achieving smaller goals along the way allows us to measure ourselves, see the progress we are making, and make adjustments if necessary.

If, at any point, you're doubting your path, stop and reflect. Consider your vision, and ask yourself — Why am I doing this? What is my purpose? When you take the time to

OUR GOALS ARE LIKE STEPPING STONES TO OUR VISION.

reengage with your purpose, you're likely to see new opportunities and ways to move forward. Your purpose is like the rudder on a boat, guiding you toward your destination. At times, you may need to adjust your course or direction, but your vision always stays in sight.

Be Flexible

When planning the next chapter of your life, be open to having it look a bit different than you might expect. Sometimes, we can get so attached to "the plan" that we overlook opportunities that are right in front of us. As I have shared, I never imagined that our move to Sonoma Wine Country would be prompted by almost losing our home in a fire.

After the Oakland Hills fire and nearly losing our house, I felt depressed, realizing how close we had come to losing everything. In the days after the fire, all I could see around our neighborhood were the burnt houses and the destruction. I felt apathetic — like nothing really mattered anymore. I would go about each day and couldn't feel the energy I usually brought to my life.

One day, I sat down with Jim and said, "I don't know what is wrong with me. I am just not happy. I don't know why. We are so fortunate we didn't lose our home." He shared that he had been feeling somewhat the same. I knew his solution when upset was to head to the garage and work on his vintage cars, which brought him a lot of satisfaction.

Our conversation made us realize that it was time to start the next chapter of our lives. It was the time for us to take action on our dream of moving to the Sonoma Wine Country. So many people had lost their homes, and selling our house would give those who had lost homes the opportunity to stay in the area and be in a home where they had friends and community. Even though the magnitude of packing everything we had and making a move seemed huge, we knew it was the right time to do it.

Jim fixed things around the house that needed updating or repair, and six months after the fire, we listed our home. It sold within weeks. A couple who had lost their home in the fire bought it, and they were willing to buy anything we wanted to leave behind. They had been living in a furnished rental apartment for six months and were eager to get their lives back. They wanted to be settled in a home and start their next chapter.

The main point here is you need to be committed and flexible. Be committed to having something happen, but also be ready for how it actually happens. Those two things don't always look the same.

Do Whatever It Takes

How many times have you wanted something so badly that you would do anything to make it work? I view that as a true measure of commitment. Settling is easy. You just rationalize that what you have is enough or that wanting more is selfish. But the reality is that there's no need to rationalize. We can create just about anything we want in life, and I have witnessed this many times throughout my years of coaching.

My best advice? Don't get stuck thinking about limitations. I have seen people give up on their dreams because they focus on all the obstacles they might face in attempting to achieve them. When my clients get stuck and are focused on the reasons why they can't have what they want, I say, "Are you a prophet? Can you see the future? How will you know unless you try?"

As a coach, I understand my clients' fear and hesitation. I take these moments to intervene and remind them of what they say they want in their life. I challenge them to remember their commitment. In times like these, people must be willing to DWIT — Do Whatever It Takes. People who focus on creating what they want in life instead of complaining about how it is, usually achieve success.

There are always possibilities in life; you just need to be open to seeing them. Focus on what is possible and stay committed to creating the future you want.

WILLINGNESS

Once you've made the commitment, you have to be willing to see it through. You'll likely have to take some risks, will undoubtedly encounter problems, and will need to be open to learning from others. These are all necessary steps to accomplish what you've committed to doing.

Be Ready for Risk

Sports always provide great metaphors. Here's a favorite — you have to risk getting off first base in order to get to second base. Anyone who loves baseball will relate to this principle of taking risks to achieve success.

I've seen this many times in work situations. A team is on track to meet its quarterly goals, but they are unwilling

YOU HAVE TO RISK GETTING OFF FIRST BASE IN ORDER TO GET TO SECOND BASE.

to push themselves to see how much further they can go. By doing what they've always done, they generally know they'll meet their baseline sales goals, so they don't feel the need to try something new to see how much more they could achieve.

The same can be true in our personal lives. We get comfortable. We may have an opportunity to make an investment, but we are afraid that we might lose the money we already have. While it is often said, "no risk, no gain," I don't know if I believe that completely. I believe in calculated risks. When I am coaching a client to take new ground in their life, regardless of the specific area we are focusing on, they often try to convince me that they are "just fine." "Fine is good," I say, "but what more do you want in your life?"

A willingness to move from where you are to where you want to go means you may need to take a risk. If you don't take it, you will never find out.

Face Problems

When I say address problems, I mean seeing a problem and jumping in with both feet to get it resolved. This commitment to solving problems distinguishes a great team from a mediocre one.

Oftentimes, people see problems but are unwilling to address them. Instead, they complain about a situation and wait for someone else to solve them. Millions of dollars in business can be lost because people are not empowered to solve problems.

On the other hand, a willingness to jump in the middle of a problem and then work to resolve it may mean you won't initially be very popular. Some problems require tough feedback and honesty to resolve them, and this may make people uncomfortable. However, the outcome can make a huge difference.

Be willing to declare a problem and then begin enrolling others to work with you to resolve it. Perhaps it means putting together an initiative and presenting it to management or having a trial to test new procedures to see if the problem can be resolved. Without commitment and action, the problem will likely continue to exist. This doesn't make anyone's job easier and, in fact, can lower productivity.

Be Coachable

Being successful requires humility. The best leaders are the best learners. They don't assume they know everything and are open to hearing different points of view rather than simply defending their position.

Aspire to this level of openness. Be willing to be coachable, and trust that you can always learn something. When you hear a different perspective or point of view, pause for a moment. Instead of saying, "Yeah, but..." to express your opinion and point of view, ask yourself the question, "What if?" and be open to the possibilities.

During San Francisco's peak dot.com period from about 1995 to 2000, the city was filled with tech startups. Young entrepreneurs were challenging the status quo and making millions of dollars from investors. Many of these companies were started by tech wizards who were able to capitalize on the beginning of the internet.

During this time, I met with one startup to discuss the value of providing the management team with coaching

THE BEST LEADERS ARE THE BEST LEARNERS.

sessions. I still remember my conversation with the founder. As I asked him what their strategic goal was, he promptly said, "To make as much money as we can."

I then asked, "But what is your long-term strategy to sustain your growth?"

He responded, "We can adapt as the market unfolds."

I left that meeting thinking, "They are in for a rude awakening." They did not see the value of coaching, and their capital infusion gave them a false sense of confidence, meaning they didn't feel the need to plan. Within two years of that meeting, eighty percent of the dot.com companies had folded, never realizing a return for their investors.

Whatever path you are on, it is always useful to seek counsel. Find an objective source who will ask you questions that may challenge your thinking and force you to look beyond current assumptions. Whenever I hear "but," I know the person I am working with is not yet ready to see a different perspective. Be willing to ask yourself the question, "What if?" and it will always lead you to a new level of awareness.

Pay It Forward

Great mentors work with people to help them develop their capabilities and professional skills by investing time with them. It's a great way to pay it forward. There are many opportunities to mentor younger people by being with them and observing what they do. Ask curious questions to help them examine their own results. Most people don't want to be told what to do, but they do respond well to some guidance and inquiry from those with experience whom they respect.

I was fortunate in my first management position to have a great mentor, Bruno Ferrioli. I always felt like he was a wise old Italian. He would come in at the end of the day, sit on the corner of my desk, and say, "Barbara, how was your day today?" At first, I was nervous, not sure what to say, but as I relaxed, I felt comfortable asking him questions about things that I was working on. He always took the time to explain things to me and would acknowledge the progress I was making as a new manager. He was an early role model for me in developing my skills as a professional coach.

Often, when coaching new managers on how to increase their bandwidth, I will hear them say, "I am so overwhelmed. I don't have time to do all that I am responsible for." Actually, this is a developmental issue. I then share the metaphor about working out at the gym. When we first start working out, the weights feel very heavy, and we are exhausted at the end of the workout. However, if we continue to work out, our muscles get stronger, and we are easily able to lift more weight.

DISCIPLINE AND PERSISTENCE = RESULTS

It is easy to get caught up in the drift of life — just going along to get along and convincing ourselves that we are fine and don't really need to create a change. We can easily talk ourselves out of things we say we want. Self-discipline is a key factor in creating success. Combined with persistence, discipline helps us stay focused and objective and allows us to assess our results consistently, without emotion. Discipline and persistence help us maintain a sense of urgency in creating what we say we want.

Objective Results

I can't tell you how many times I have shared with clients my belief that the physical universe is the ultimate teacher. The slowest gazelle in the herd gets eaten by the lion. No judgment. It just is what it is. When my clients are beating around the bush, explaining why they have the results and outcomes they have, I often say, "Rocks are hard, and water is wet. The universe is the ultimate guru." There's no debate that rocks are hard and water is wet. These are simply objective facts.

Many times, people will avoid looking at results objectively. When we don't achieve our goals, it is so easy to blame the circumstances or someone else's actions. But if we look at the situation objectively, we can see more clearly what was missing — what was needed to be successful. We must get out of reaction and judgment modes in order to see our results in this way.

When clients talk about results in subjective terms, I usually ask, "How can you measure this?" Effectiveness is generally based on objective results. In fact, there is a certain freedom when looking at your life objectively. Ambiguity and uncertainty make it difficult to see new opportunities. Sometimes, when I feel stuck or I'm not moving forward, I ask myself, "Is this the way I want my life to be now?" With that question, I look objectively at how I have been spending my time and what I might be avoiding.

It's easy to get caught up in judging ourselves or comparing ourselves to others. Years before I turned fifty, I remember saying to a friend, "I will be so glad when I turn fifty. I won't care what anyone thinks. I will stop worrying about

THE PHYSICAL UNIVERSE IS THE ULTIMATE TEACHER.

how I look or how much money I make. I will just get to let myself be who I am." Well, that didn't happen, but my focus did shift a great deal. I started spending more time looking objectively at what I was creating in my life and less time judging myself and my actions.

It is easy to blame ourselves or make excuses, but this is not the path to success and self-confidence. Owning what you are creating puts you in a powerful place. By looking objectively at your results, you will feel lighter and better able to take action.

Urgency Versus Desperation

When designing your next chapter, I suggest you have some urgency about it. Of course, spend time determining where you want to go, but once that's decided, get going. Having a sense of urgency creates excitement and commitment, which leads to action. A great plan, if not executed, will never bring you what you want.

If we lack focus, it can be easy to simply react to situations based on the circumstances. We may even get desperate or fearful, not trusting ourselves or the choices we have made. This type of desperation is a form of scarcity. It is like looking at your future through a long, narrow tube. It closes down your peripheral vision, so you are unable to see all the opportunities you have around you.

One year, my accountant told me that, for tax purposes, I should get a new car. To get the most benefit, I was supposed to purchase one before the end of the year, but I kept putting it off. It was too cold and rainy outside. I was too busy. It was almost the end of the year when Jim and I finally drove to a

A GREAT PLAN, IF NOT EXECUTED, WILL NEVER BRING YOU WHAT YOU WANT.

nearby dealership. We had owned a Nissan hybrid, and I was interested in something a little sportier. I went out for a test-drive in a Volkswagen Passat with the salesperson while Jim stayed behind at the dealership.

After about twenty minutes of driving, I turned the car to head back to the dealership. At that moment, I was struck sideways and T-boned by another driver who was attempting to pass me. In an instant, the car was filled with smoke. The airbag had deployed, and my down jacket had been ripped open by my seat belt, sending feathers flying. I was in shock. The poor salesperson who had been sitting next to me in the passenger seat began screaming, "Get out! Get out!" But I couldn't move. I was blocked in and unable to open the door. The police and ambulance came.

For the next few weeks, we dealt with the dealership's insurance. The car was totaled, but we were not at fault. I felt so guilty. I almost went back to buy a car from the same dealer, but I was still in shock from the accident. By this time, I had become desperate to get a new car before the end of the year, but the last thing I wanted to do was test-drive another car.

In the end, I went to a Nissan dealer and bought the latest model of the same car we had before — without even test-driving it. Even though we had gotten a new car, I was never really happy with it because I had purchased it out of desperation rather than with clarity about what I really wanted.

When we take time to become clear about what we want and what our purpose is, it is easier to make decisions. We know when to say yes and when to say no. Failing to create a plan and take action to execute the plan leads to desperation.

Details, Discipline, and Persistence

You've read about many principles of accomplishment in this chapter, but this one supports almost every single one — attention to detail, a disciplined approach, and genuine persistence when confronting challenges. Embodying these qualities creates excellence.

As a coach, I work with clients to incorporate these elements into their vision and daily actions. When I think of persistence, I always think of one young company I worked with that had a vision of someday becoming a publicly held company. First, they needed to get seed funding in order to develop their product and bring it to market.

We've all read success stories of how companies get funding, develop a product, and grow to profitability. What most people don't realize is that there are many more companies that never achieve success. Getting seed money is not easy, even in the best of times.

The CEO of this company worked hard to write a compelling story for investors. Appointments were set up, and presentations were made. With each presentation, there was the excitement that this would be the one that would enroll in their story and provide the funding that was needed. But weeks went by, and then months.

The team continued to work on developing the product, working long hours without pay and believing that the money would soon come in. Small personal loans and credit cards were used to cover expenses. At one point, the CEO was exhausted and shared, "I have to give it up. This isn't going to work." As much as they believed in the product, there were no promissory notes being offered by investors.

"What haven't you tried yet?" I asked.

"I think I have tried everything. I can't think of anything else to do," he said.

I said, "There must be something."

"I think I just need to take a break and get some rest," he said. During that break, the call came in. One of the investment groups was ready to meet and make a deal. It is always darkest before the dawn.

Discipline can be hard to maintain, but it is a key element of success. I believe this to be true. It makes me a little crazy when I hear someone comment, "They sure got lucky," about a person who has been successful multiple times. It is never about luck. It is about having the self-discipline and persistence to keep pursuing the goals that made them successful.

I coached a young man at one point who played a very valuable role for a consulting company. He had decided that he wanted to start his own company and make money to put in his pocket instead of the company that he was working for. He hired me to work with him to set up and start his own company. As we worked together to develop his business plan and the financials, he began to see the work that would be required to run his own company. He realized that he would be responsible for paying employees month after month, securing contracts, and managing teams and the accounts they would have.

As he approached the time to make the decision to leave his job, he shared with me, "I know I could be successful having my own company, but I realize now that I would need to give up a lot of freedom and the personal time I now have to spend with my family. My kids are young, and I don't really want to miss time with them."

"Yes," I said, "it will take a lot of your time. You will need to have a lot of self-discipline, manage a lot of details, and be persistent in finding new accounts for your team."

In the end, he decided to remain at the company he was working for. After he had done the hard work and research, he realized the level of self-discipline and commitment that would be required to run his own company. He decided he could be successful in his current role and had a renewed commitment to the company he was working for. He was glad to share the profits with his employer now, realizing all that they did to support him in the work that he was doing.

Accomplishing your goals will require commitment, planning, flexibility, and persistence. There are no shortcuts. But if you have the discipline to work through the process, you will have a greater chance of success in achieving the outcome that is right for you.

BEING RESPONSIBLE FOR CARING FOR OURSELVES IS THE GREATEST GIFT WE CAN GIVE TO OTHERS.

CHAPTER 11

SELF-CARE DURING CHANGE

When we take time to care for ourselves, we are able to contribute more to those around us. Change can be stressful, and we've been discussing a lot of changes. Even if the goal is a good one, the process can be challenging. To that end, it's essential that you develop effective ways to manage stress by committing to self-care. Many simple things can make a difference — maintaining a healthy mindset, communicating with people close to you, and accepting love. These habits will keep you engaged in the process and prevent you from isolating yourself. Work to be optimistic about your future and set short-term goals to move forward.

For most of my life, I have been a deadline player. I found it exciting to get to the finish line of a project just in time. I've also always been a multitasker with the capacity to juggle many things without getting too stressed. However, as I have gotten older, I've noticed that operating in this way is not as fun or fulfilling. I prefer to have things lined up and prioritized, but things don't always line up.

In the process of navigating change, there are typically things that we are unable to predict. We are going down unfamiliar roads, and the feeling of uncertainty can drain our energy. Meeting new people, starting a new job, managing finances in a new way, or ending a relationship can leave us feeling fatigued, stressed, and confused. During these times, it's even more essential to have personal practices in place that will help us stay grounded, clear on our purpose, and focused on values.

Instead, many people try to get through this period by using stimulants, alcohol, or food to deal with their emotions, which does not really help the situation. Lack of sleep or too much sleep are also not helpful ways of managing difficult times.

HEALTHY HABITS

During the "Now What?" phase of change, I encourage people to make time to engage in healthy habits — starting a new exercise program, hobby, sport, or practice that supports their spiritual being. Other healthy pursuits include things like participating in community service activities or just staying connected with friends. People can become consumed by the challenge of change. By creating time to shift their focus, they can become more objective and neutral about what they are going through.

Stay with me because this may feel like the exact opposite of what you want to do. However, letting go and creating time to relax and reflect can be healing and helpful. Take moments for serenity. Surround yourself with the beauty of nature — notice the sky and birds flying by, and practice grounding yourself.

I figured this one out the hard way. Many years ago, I was working on the president's staff in San Francisco. I was a new member of the strategic planning team, and I was very stressed trying to do everything right, fitting in with the new team, and managing deadlines. One afternoon, I called Jim, who was working down the street in another corporate office. I said, "I am so stressed. I feel like I can barely breathe."

He said, "Get up from your desk, go down to the street, and take a walk around the block. Get some fresh air to clear your head."

I said, " I can't do that. I have too much work to do."

"Yes, you can," he said.

Reluctantly, I got up, went down the elevator, and walked out onto the busy streets of San Francisco. As I walked around the block, I could feel the coolness of the ocean breeze from the Bay on my face, and it began to clear my head. I looked around and noticed other people out on the street. Many were tourists visiting the city and enjoying time with their families. Others, like me, were business people walking to meetings. Slowly, my stress and anxiety began to slip away. I returned to my office refreshed and with a clear head.

What I had been working on no longer seemed so hard. This taught me an important lesson. Move your body, and your mind will follow.

MOVE YOUR BODY, AND YOUR MIND WILL FOLLOW.

SELF-CARE STRATEGIES

Taking a walk is just one of many self-care strategies out there. In this section, I'll go over some other great options.

Try doing some **Brain Gym exercises** to wake up your brain. Brain gym exercises are based on the idea that specific movements can improve brain function.[16]

Take a **movement or dance break**. Put on some fun, high-energy music and stand up. Practice left and right leg crossovers. Swing your arms and rotate from your waist or march in place for thirty seconds. The point is to just start moving. At the end of your high-energy song, you will feel refreshed and more alert than you did before you started.

Meditation has proven psychological, physical, and spiritual effects. Through meditation, we become less concerned about our material life and begin to experience value in the environment that we create around us while developing a stronger sense of well-being. When our body is healthy and functioning at an optimum level, we have more energy, experience less stress, and have more positive thoughts.

I tried for many years to meditate but never felt like I "got it." But I love to walk in nature, and that worked for me. I would clear my mind and just "be" without any thoughts running through my mind. I focused on smells and sounds as I walked and relaxed. Years later, I learned that there actually was such a thing as "walking meditation," which is what I had been doing.

Yoga also has proven psychological, physical, and spiritual benefits. I lead a leadership training course in our community. As part of the training, participants are asked to work as a team to align on and execute a Make a Difference (MAD) project.

The leaders of one group were inspired by a local woman with Parkinson's who was leading a yoga group. They were impressed with her commitment to continue to do this work in light of her physical limitations. She shared with them that practicing yoga on a regular basis helps individuals maintain their balance and increases their peace of mind in dealing with this disease.

The group decided to hold a fundraiser to raise funds for the Michael J. Fox Foundation and to help educate the community on the value of yoga in fighting this limiting disease. They raised fifty thousand dollars in ten weeks and held a concert and yoga event for three hundred people.

Journaling is another effective way to stay connected with our emotions and create space to reflect on how we are experiencing the changes in our lives. It provides quiet time away from distractions. Journaling can be an outlet for self-expression and provides time to connect with what is authentically true for us. It always helps to reflect on our values and priorities in life and express gratitude for what we have. During some of the most challenging times of change, it is powerful to spend time reflecting on what you are grateful for. "I am alive. I am healthy. I am secure. I have friends to support me."

Resolutions are another way people commit to self-care habits, especially at the start of the year. Many make declarations and resolutions about what they are committed to changing or accomplishing in the year ahead. We may do the same when we start a new chapter in our lives.

One year, a friend told me, "I am going to lose fifty pounds. I am going to start walking, stop eating out, and cook healthy foods." Since we frequently chatted, I would listen to what she was doing that supported her declaration. "I went grocery shopping today and bought a lot of good, healthy fruits and vegetables." she said, then added, "Boy, grocery shopping is a lot of work." Not wanting to be judgmental by saying, "Everyone goes grocery shopping!" I told her that was great news, and I was sure she would get used to it.

After a few weeks, I asked her how her daily walking routine was going. She told me that she had been walking consistently but had not seen any results in her weight. "Well," I said, "It will take time. You are probably developing muscle, and muscle weighs more than fat."

Early in the spring, she decided to book a tour to Japan, a place she had always wanted to see. When we connected, she shared how amazing the food was and how much she enjoyed the trip. She declared that she was going to spend as much time traveling as possible. Travel had always been her passion, and now that she was retired, she could do as much as she liked. As the months passed, many trips were booked — New York City, Belgium, Costa Rica, Florida, and Thailand.

Because we have been friends for over thirty years, I did not nag her about her declaration of home cooking, exercise, and eating healthy. She was enjoying herself. But at the end of that year, she had a health scare. She realized that being healthy was really important and that she had not been keeping her resolution. Now, she is taking her life on with a commitment to being healthy, traveling, and enjoying life. She is living her best life and also practicing self-care at the same time.

Everyone knows that self-care is important. However, sometimes, it can take a scare before we realize how important it is and begin to make changes in our lives.

CREATING BALANCE

People often tell me they want to create more balance in their lives. I believe that balance in life is an oxymoron. Nothing in life ever stays in balance. What I coach people to understand is that they have the capacity to respond to different situations in their lives.

I like to use the metaphor of the wobbleboard that we stand on in the gym to practice keeping our bodies in balance. Just when you adjust your posture and get centered on top of the board, it moves below you. But we still manage to stay on top of it without falling off. We cannot keep everything in balance all the time, but we can adapt and shift from moment to moment based on what is happening around us.

When we are under stress and confronting changes, it's important to make choices that maintain balance in our lives. This can provide us with the inner resources to stay resilient and adaptable. Physics teaches us that in any system, the element with the most flexibility will be the controlling element. This is especially true in our daily lives. When we practice self-care, we develop the flexibility and capability to adjust to the changes that are occurring around us.

PRIORITIZE YOURSELF

Begin to notice what makes you feel good and allow yourself to spend time doing these activities. Put time for yourself on your calendar and commit to it. Do not let another appointment or event interrupt the time you have committed

PHYSICS TEACHES US THAT IN ANY SYSTEM, THE ELEMENT WITH THE MOST FLEXIBILITY WILL BE THE CONTROLLING ELEMENT.

to yourself. Commitments to yourself are just as important as commitments to others.

Also, be kind to yourself. Starting a new chapter takes a lot of energy. As part of this process, we are often required to meet new people — a new job, a new location, or a change in our relationships. For many, this feels like starting over and can be a bit intimidating – but that's okay. Try to find the fun in it, and cut yourself some slack when it feels hard.

Learning to engage socially in a new environment can feel awkward. I like to remind myself that we are more alike than different and that most people are looking for connections with others. This empowers me to reach out and meet new people. Here are some ways to do this:

- Take a vacation or tour with a group of like-minded people.
- Join a gym or golf club.
- Join a support group to talk through the issues you are facing.
- Start communicating in your local community in chat groups.
- Clear out the clutter in your home and host a yard sale.
- Go to a local comedy club and get a good laugh. It will increase your endorphins and help you gain a new perspective on your life.
- Join a craft or art group.

Take time for yourself and recognize that it can look many different ways. As I have aged, I have found different ways to practice self-care than what I did when I was younger. As with any exercise program, it is always good to occasionally change up your routine. Don't get stuck in a rut. Find new ways to practice self-care.

The more you practice self-care, the more you will enjoy being around others, and the more they will enjoy you.

TO EVERYTHING, THERE IS A SEASON.

—THE BYRDS.
"Turn! Turn! Turn!"

CHAPTER *12*

THE SEASONS OF CHANGE

The thing about change is that it never ends. Even if we try to avoid it, change will always be a part of life, both at home and at work.

I have faith that my life will move on and that Jim's spirit will always be with me. A few days after Jim passed, my friend suggested we take a trip to the coast to get away for a few days. Feeling the full impact of my grief, I held on to the faith I had that Jim was in a better place and that I had done everything to make his transition as beautiful and comfortable as possible.

While I knew he was gone and my life would change, I received many signs that he was with me. I talked to God and went to church. The priest began his sermon with the verse from Ecclesiastes 3:1-8, which is also reflected in the lyrics of the song "Turn! Turn! Turn!" sung by the Byrds, a musical group from my generation.[17] I remembered the lyrics as he spoke about the seasons of change. I felt a calm come over me, knowing that I was exactly where I needed to be to heal.

As you consider the changes you have had in your life and how you have moved through them, you may begin to recognize and reflect on similarities with what I have shared with you in this book. I want you to know that we all have seasons and times of change to go through. We have the capability to evolve and to create what we want. No matter how change comes at us, we all get to choose the "now what" for our lives.

Turn! Turn! Turn!

> To everything, turn, turn, turn
> There is a season turn, turn, turn
> And a time to every purpose under Heaven
>
> A time to be born, a time to die,
> A time to plant, a time to reap.
> A time to kill, a time to heal,
> A time to laugh, a time to weep.
>
> A time to build up, a time to break down
> A time to dance, a time to mourn
> A time to cast away stones,
> A time to gather stones together.
>
> A time of love, a time of hate,
> A time of war, a time of peace.
> A time you may embrace,
> A time to refrain from embracing.

A time to gain, a time to lose,
A time to rain, a time to sow
A time for love, a time for hate
A time for peace, I swear it's not too late

If I could go back and have a conversation with that little girl who stood in the sun against the red brick wall in the schoolyard years ago, I would tell her about all the changes she would make in her life and the difference she would make in the world. I would share with her all the good she would create and the wisdom she would share because of her experiences and commitment to being different.

She got her first job the way she did because she wanted to start her young life differently than others. She became a young manager because of her commitment to working hard, proving herself, and doing her best. She was courageous enough to be a manager of over one hundred and fifty construction workers who told her they could never work for a woman. She was selected for the leadership team that helped to determine the future of the "Baby Bells" after the breakup of AT&T.

She was brave enough to leave a successful corporate career, call herself a business coach, and then become a pioneer in the coaching profession for the next thirty years.

She bravely faced breast cancer and four joint replacements before the age of sixty-five, and she had the strength to go through the caregiving of her husband, providing compassion and love until his final day.

The woman who achieved these things would never have existed if she hadn't been told that she was gifted by her fourth-grade teacher and then went on to believe in herself and surround herself with people who also saw her gifts and passion for learning and giving to others.

And she wouldn't have married a man who positively reinforced her every day of his life — a husband who used to tell his friends, "The day I try to put a bit in her mouth is the day I will lose her." Smart man, my husband. I will be eternally grateful that he found me in the middle of a construction and engineering yard in Fresno, managing crews of men, and seeing in me a woman who was willing to be different and who would later become the love of his life.

Next Chapters

So now I am designing the next chapter of my life using all the resources I have collected over the years to guide me. The resources I have shared with you in this book are designed to make each transition of your life an opportunity for new learning and an opening for new possibilities.

Every generation has its own set of challenges to face. I have been fortunate enough to live in two centuries and to see the technology revolution of the twentieth century unfold — from the first black and white TV being delivered to our home when I was five to seeing Pacific Bell place the first fiber optic loop around Los Angeles, making internet access available for the Olympics in 1984.

The world has come out of the shutdown created by COVID-19, and each of us has learned many lessons. For me, the lessons were patience, trusting myself more than I have ever done in my life, and learning to ask for support. With each new chapter in life, we take what we have learned from the past and bring that knowledge into our future.

I am sure that the lessons of the first three years of the 2020s will not be lost on the Millennials, Gen Z, and their heirs. These were life-defining times in which every human being on the planet was engaged in and impacted by COVID. The lessons learned will shape the way we respond to change in the future. We may go back to some of the behaviors that we had before this pandemic, but things will never be the same.

We have innovated, found a deeper part of ourselves, learned to set priorities, and taken more responsibility for the quality of our lives.

Stay Curious

I often use a growth metaphor with my clients, "When you are green, you are growing. When you are ripe, you start to rot. The challenge is to stay green, curious, expanding, and open to learning and new discoveries."

In the Sonoma Wine Country, we see the seasons change by watching the cycle of the vines. In the winter, the vines are bare, like skeletons in the field. After the rains at the beginning of spring, they break bud, and you can just begin to see a hint of green. As the weather warms and summer approaches, you can see the vines growing at a rapid rate and brilliant fields of green for miles. As summer fades, the grape clusters grow and fill with sugar. When the time is right, the harvest begins, collecting tons of grapes before the rains come and the leaves start to turn dark and shed, preparing for winter.

Our lives are like the seasons in nature. As we grow and mature, we change in order to create the "Now what?" in our lives. With each new "Now what?" we have choices — get married, buy a house, develop as a professional, have children, travel, continue our education, invest in something that we believe will yield a good return, and so many more.

Resilience

With each new "Now What?" we also recognize that we are responsible for creating what we want. We have choices and get to make them. Perhaps we don't always like the choices we have, but we still get to choose. It is with that knowledge that we accept the challenge to change and design a life that brings us joy and fulfillment. People are resilient. No matter what life throws at us, we have the ability to adapt.

None of us goes through life alone. Learning to reach out and utilize all the available resources means letting go of our pride, ego, or whatever stops us from asking for help. After doing this, we can manifest change, not just in our own lives but in the world.

As human beings, we have changed our world so many times and in so many ways. I believe each individual has the resilience to change their life into one that brings them a sense of joy, fulfillment, and connection with others.

As the lyrics from the *Hamilton* musical say, "There's a million things I haven't done. Just you wait."[18] I am not done yet. There are many things I still want to do and see. I intend to move forward, explore new places, meet new people, and continue to learn new things. Whatever your next chapter is, I hope this book helps you design and navigate it. We never know what the next day will bring, but we must be willing to believe that there will be another day, and we have the power to make it great.

Our world will continue to change in both positive ways and ways that will challenge us to adapt and change (as we learned in the 2020s). Whatever changes occur, we are resilient and can adapt to what is happening in our lives and the world around us.

So What Do You Want? Now What Is Possible?

We can use the resources we have to manage and even thrive, creating a positive experience that we might not have imagined in the beginning.

We have our past, the experiences we have had, and the lessons we have learned, which, over time, become our wisdom. By applying what we have learned and seeing the value each of us contributes from our unique perspectives, we can create so many new opportunities.

Always remember that you count and that without you in the world, it would not be the same. With each new chapter, you bring your lessons and your views of what is possible.

Live life with a clear purpose and values. Understand that it is no accident that you are here at this time in the world. Each of us is meant to make a difference and leave our mark on the world. Continue to envision your future, get clear about what you want, get committed to it, and declare it. Get out of your comfort zone and enroll resources around you to help you create it. Lastly, celebrate each day. Be in gratitude for all that you have and all that you are able to contribute to the world around you.

Acknowledge the people in your life whom you love and who love you. Take time to be with them and celebrate with them. We make a lot of assumptions about people — what they are doing and what we think they want. Instead, make the time to check in with people to find out what they are really doing and what they really want. As we evolve, our needs change, our habits change, and the way we choose to spend time changes. Never get to the end of a year or a day feeling like it wasn't what you wanted.

You have the freedom to declare what you want so that you can see, hear, and experience the people around you. You have the power to make requests of others and ask for what you want.

At each phase of your life, keep asking yourself these questions — So what change do I want? Now what is possible? Do not hesitate to be different. Being different is what makes you unique, and it can inspire others to take ownership and pride in all the ways they are unique and different.

I hope to see many of you down the road. As I complete this book, it is a milestone in my next chapter. Now, it is time to get out there. It's time to meet the many people I wrote this book for and ask them — So what? Now what?

ENDNOTES

1. Clare Josa, *Ditching The Imposter Syndrome*, (United Kingdom: Beyond Alchemy Publishing, 2020).
2. Anna Quindlen, *Being Perfect* (New York: Random House, 2005).
3. Stephanie Rosenbloom. "Authentic? Get Real." *New York Times*, September 11, 2011.
4. Sarah Ban Breathnach, *Something More: Excavating Your Authentic Self*, (New York: Grand Central Publishing, 1998).
5. Margery Williams, *The Velveteen Rabbit* (New York: Doubleday & Company, 1921).
6. M. Scott Peck, M.D., *The Road Less Traveled*, (New York: Simon and Schuster, 1978).
7. *2020 ICF Global Coaching Study Executive Summary*, International Coaching Federation.
8. Brian Tracy, *Eat That Frog*, (London: Hodder Paperbacks, 2013).
9. Stephen R Covey, *The Seven Habits of Highly Effective People*, (New York: Simon and Schuster, 1989).
10. Robert E Quinn, *Building the Bridge as You Walk on It*, (San Francisco: Jossey-Bass, 2004).
11. Joseph Campbell (1904-1987) was an American writer and professor of literature at Sarah Lawrence College in comparative mythology and comparative religion.

12 Virginia Satir (1916 – 1988) was an American author, researcher, and psychotherapist.
13 Peter Lencioni, *Five Dysfunctions of a Team* (Hoboken: Jossey-Bass, 2002).
14 Stephen Covey, *Seven Habits of Highly Effective People* (New York: Simon and Schuster, 1989).
15 Plato, *Plato's The Republic* (New York: Books, Inc., 1943).
16 Brain Gym was founded in 1987 by Paul and Gail Dennison.
17 The Byrds, "Turn! Turn! Turn!" (1965). Pete Seeger, composer.
18 *Hamilton: An American Musical* (2015), composer Lin-Manuel Miranda.

THANK YOU

I want to thank each and every student I have trained in the last twenty years — many of you have become the Professional Performance Coaches you were intended to be. Together, you gently rock the world to create change and opportunities for people and organizations, helping them grow, expand their capabilities, and make a difference. Each of you has inspired me to become the best coach and mentor I can possibly be and motivated me to continue to learn new ways of empowering commitment.

I am eternally grateful to Dana Simons. Her love and faith have provided me with a soft place to land, and she challenged me to keep my promise in writing this book as a way to heal and begin to realize my next chapter.

My BFF for over thirty years, Lou Dozier, has been with me, up and down and all around. In 1987, Lou, Jim, and I became like the characters in *Three's Company*. Together, we support each other one hundred percent to be our very best and will continue to do so until the end of the road. Lou and I are now Thelma and Louise, both starting our next chapter and making every day count.

Thank you to Nicole Gebhardt and the team at Niche Pressworks for their coaching and support. I could not have gotten to this point without their excellent guidance.

MEET BARBARA FAGAN

After reading this book, I hope you have an understanding of who I am and what I do. I am committed to taking a strong stand for positive change with the people and organizations I work with. I believe in the potential of every human being and that we are all capable of creating what we want in life. I have been known for my professional integrity and my quick and witty "zaps of truth," which my clients tell me can move mountains of resistance.

I left AT&T in 1987 after twenty years of work, and I was still under the age of forty. With my experience in almost every aspect of business, I began coaching organizations involved in creating products and services in the new technology arena. I have had the opportunity to coach clients on their strategic direction and through change initiatives, as well as individuals facing life-changing situations. I continue to learn about change with every client.

By 2003, I had spent over 20,000 hours coaching individuals and organizations. I decided to develop the Certified Professional Coach Curriculum and began to train and certify professional coaches. Since then, I have continued to deliver this program and our leadership training throughout the United States, Mexico, Taiwan, Hong Kong, and Greater China. Source Point Training programs are accredited to the highest level, with both the International Association for Coaching headquartered in London and the International Coach Federation (ICF) in the United States.

I enjoy gardening, spending time with friends and family around the world, and being home with my fur family. For the past thirty years, I've lived in Healdsburg, California, in Sonoma County, where I enjoy the changing seasons, the beauty of nature around me, and a community that provides great healing and restoration.

PAYING IT FORWARD

Change can happen suddenly, with little time to prepare, and creating the next chapter of our life can be scary. When moving from one chapter in life to another, it sometimes feels lonely until we get to the place we want to be. At times, it will feel like we are starting over.

Change requires courage and commitment. As a coach with over thirty years of experience, my purpose is to support others to help them create positive change in their life. I teach them tools that allow them to begin to see possibilities for themselves so they can live a fulfilling and joyful life.

As you read this book, perhaps you are thinking of someone you know who is also facing a change in their life. If you would like to help them, you can let them know about this book and invite them to read it. When people realize they are not alone and that others have taken a similar journey, they are empowered to move forward and create the same thing for themselves.

You can make a difference for someone by introducing them to this book and the resources that it provides. THANK YOU in advance for your contribution to others.

TO LEARN MORE ABOUT SOURCE POINT TRAINING:

🌐 Website: SourcePointTraining.com

✉ Email: Barbara@SourcePointTraining.com

COACHING PROGRAMS:

- Coaching Fundamentals and Mastery
- Leadership Skills and Tools
- Business Team Coaching
- Certified Relationship Coaching

CORPORATE RETREATS AND STRATEGIC PLANNING WORKSHOPS/SEMINARS:

- Living A Life of Purpose
- Creating Vision and Abundance
- Speaking Engagements
- Designing The Next Chapter of Your Life

Made in the USA
Middletown, DE
05 May 2024